10
Important Things Your
Driving Instructor Never Taught You –
To Make You a Better Driver

Also available by Peter Russell
from Bloomsbury Publishing plc

**10 Main Reasons for Failing the Driving Test –
and how to avoid them**
ISBN: 0 7475 1628 6

How to Pass the Written Driving Test
ISBN: 0 7475 2500 5

10
Important Things Your Driving Instructor Never Taught You – To Make You a Better Driver

PETER RUSSELL

BLOOMSBURY

The information in this book was correct to the best of the editor's and publisher's belief at the time of going to press. While no responsibility can be accepted for errors and omissions, the editor and publisher would welcome corrections and suggestions for material to include in subsequent editions of this book.

First published in 1996 by
Bloomsbury Publishing plc
2 Soho Square
London, W1V 6HB

A copy of the CIP entry for this book is available from the British Library

ISBN 0 7475 2501 3

10 9 8 7 6 5 4 3 2 1

Typeset by Hewer Text Composition Services, Edinburgh
Printed and bound in Great Britain by
Clays Limited, St Ives Plc

Contents

Contents

Introduction

Does experience help drivers avoid accidents?

The simple answer is YES. But if you reword the question by asking: 'Do drivers get better as they get more experienced?' the answer has to be NO! This is because most people's experience only enables them to avoid accidents at the last moment − if they're lucky, and have quick reactions, they usually manage to draw back from the final confrontation. New drivers, especially those driving beyond their limited skills, can easily find themselves into − and stuck with − that final confrontation before they realize it. Experienced drivers can often rely on their ability to handle their vehicle well in a panic to get them out of difficulties: new drivers don't have this skill yet. They need to think themselves out of trouble before it starts.

When you passed your driving test the driving examiner gave you two pieces of paper. One was the pass certificate. The other was the marking sheet, which often contains a number of items marked with a stroke like this /. Don't ignore this minor marking. Knowing what you did wrong, and avoiding repeating it, might save your life one day.

As a new driver you need to practise the following in order to gain the experience to keep you safe.

- See what is going on all around you.
- Tell other road users what you are going to do.
- Adjust your position and speed to suit your needs.

- Keep a 'safety cushion' around you at all times.
- Keep your vehicle in good condition.
- Keep yourself in good health and fit to drive – safely at all times.

Incidents

Accidents do not just happen: road-traffic accidents, as they are known by the police and media, are badly named. They should be recognized as incidents. The word 'accident' implies that they are no one's fault. They all have a simple and similar cause. Two road users try to occupy the same piece of road, or a driver tries to put his vehicle into a space already occupied by a lamppost, wall, or ditch. Good drivers recognize the build-up before they reach that stage and try to avoid the final conclusion.

Unfortunately this is where experience fails us all. Minor errors happen all the time. The problems only occur when two people make a minor error together, so drivers have learned to live – and sometimes die – with them. But minor errors can be fatal, especially when they are ignored, or drivers aren't aware that they're making them.

All incidents start with a *vulnerability*. Most drivers make themselves vulnerable all the time they are driving, and in the driving test driving examiners mark these vulnerabilities as minor errors, shown by / on the marking sheet. They don't fail, they are simply noted in passing. If two road users make themselves vulnerable at the same time – and close to each other – they create a *confrontation*. Good drivers are usually able to resolve the confrontation without it going further, but if left unresolved the confrontation rapidly becomes a *crisis*. Lucky drivers can sometimes extricate themselves from a crisis too. But if they don't, the next step is the *crunch*. When the incident involves only one road user making himself vulnerable, the confrontation and crisis develop so quickly the crunch follows automatically.

There is a logic in this so simple that you should put it into practice all the time. If you never have a crisis you can't have a crunch. If you never have a confrontation you can't have a crisis. If you never make yourself vulnerable you can't have a confrontation. *Never make yourself vulnerable; always avoid other people's vulnerabilities.*

The safety cushion

Everyone must have a 'safety cushion', a safe space all around their vehicle, when they are driving. What minimum gap do you need between you and the vehicle ahead?

The answer which most good drivers will give you is simple. Many quote or paraphrase the Highway Code.

> **HC 57**
> **Drive at a speed that will allow you to stop well within the distance you can see to be clear.**

Others quote the various forms of safe distances which drivers are advised to keep from each other: the two-second rule; one foot, or one yard, for every mile an hour; one car length for every 10 m.p.h. The really clever ones can even quote the braking distances at each speed from 20–70 m.p.h.

Miles per hour	Thinking distance		Braking distance		Total stopping distance		
	m	ft	m	ft	m	ft	car lengths
20	6	20	6	20	12	40	3 car lengths
30	9	30	14	45	23	75	6 car lengths
40	12	40	24	80	36	120	9 car lengths
50	15	50	38	125	53	175	13 car lengths
60	18	60	55	180	73	240	18 car lengths
70	21	70	75	245	96	315	24 car lengths

Some drivers will just look blankly at you. These are the ones who have just driven the past ten minutes, ten miles, or even ten years glued firmly to the rear bumper of the vehicle in front. This raises the question why do so many drivers break all these rules? Even drivers who can give the correct answers about braking and stopping distances still drive too closely. The answer is that experience teaches them that you can get away with breaking rules most of the time. So experience is not such a good teacher as you might think.

The safest drivers are sometimes those who have just learned a very cheap but salutary lesson from experience. Cheap – because it never went past the crisis stage. Salutary – because for a brief moment the driver recognized the fact that the crunch was avoided by outside circumstances or through someone else's skills and reactions. For a few days they will drive really well. They will maintain a much safer following distance than before and their eyes peeled as they concentrate on the driving task as if their very lives depended upon it. The really safe, competent and proficient driver is the one who practises ample following distances all the time, taking into account road and weather conditions, and who always allows that little bit extra – just in case.

What causes accidents on the road?

Driver error
Driver error is the greatest single cause of road-traffic accidents: it is the major cause in 98% of them and the only cause in over 85%.

The first three main errors which are made by all drivers at times, which must eventually lead to loss of control or collision, are:

- Following too closely.
- Turning right unsafely.
- Trying to overtake when it is not safe.

The next seven errors are:

- Travelling faster than the main stream of traffic.
- Driving too fast into bends.
- Swinging wide on bends.
- Driving too close to parked or slower-moving road users.
- Failing to give way when required.
- Giving wrong signals or giving none at all.
- Making wrong assumptions about other road users.

Each of these errors starts out as a minor fault. If you continue to make minor errors, especially the same ones repeatedly, then it won't be long before someone else joins you in your vulnerability. You cannot rely on other people keeping out of your way for ever.

Following too closely

Most non-drivers, asked what the major cause of accidents on the road is, answer emotively: *speed*. Some go much further and take as their sole message the ambiguous one that speed kills. They argue that by cutting down speed accidents are reduced, and no one is killed. There is about as much truth in this idea as in the opposite view, which was suggested by a noted road-safety enthusiast who stated that as roads get narrower because of roadworks, parked cars, and other obstructions so drivers should increase their speed to maintain the same traffic flow.

Both are wrong – tragically the greatest single driver error causing road-traffic incidents is *tailgating*, or drivers following each other too closely. These drivers have a warped idea, based on lots of experience when nothing actually went wrong, that they can always stop in the distance they're following behind the vehicle ahead. This distance is always safe provided that the vehicle ahead slows down gracefully, and pulls up some twenty, thirty, or more metres further on. What they can't cope with is when it stops suddenly. That's when the tailgating vulture comes home to roost.

Skilful, safe driving

Lack of concentration on the task in hand is always dangerous; excessive speed becomes the final ingredient needed to make the accident serious.

Excessive speed is always a question of drivers using speed that is excessive in relation to what is happening around them. Good driving doesn't mean driving slowly, and it certainly doesn't mean driving more slowly than those around you. Your two choices at all times must be to select the correct position in the road, and to travel at the safest speed.

A skilful and safe driver is one who can judge the safest position and speed for the conditions at any time. The skill of staying safe is to keep a safety cushion all round you. Drive at the same speed as the traffic flow in your lane or on your road; if there are no other vehicles around you, such as when you're driving on country lanes, make sure you can readily stop before the next bend, entrance, or obstacle.

Safe driver's quiz

Tick the answer which is closest to what you think?

1 Under normal driving conditions you should be looking and planning what you intend to do for at least

a   2 seconds ahead.
b   4 seconds ahead.
c   10 seconds ahead.
d   20 seconds ahead.

2   Right of way, when applied to driving on the roads,

a   is always given to the traffic on the main road.
b   only applies to traffic turning left into side roads.
c   should be given to people emerging on your left.
d   does not exist, as you can only give priority.

3   You wish to overtake a large truck on a three-lane single carriageway in a 50 m.p.h. limit. What position should you take up in relation to it?

a   As close as you can before moving out.
b   About two car lengths before moving out.
c   Move out from about ten car lengths before deciding to pass.
d   Move out from ten car lengths and get past as soon as possible.

4   It has been a long, hot summer, and today there is the first light shower of rain for a long time. What is the greatest danger to a new driver?

a   Being dazzled by oncoming vehicles' lights.
b   The road becoming very greasy and slippery.
c   The brake drums getting wet and needing drying out.
d   Being distracted by the wipers making a noise.

5   You have just bought a second-hand car and you're not sure if the tyres are legal. Which one of the following would be legal?

a   The tread depth on one of the tyres is only 2.6 mm.
b   A cross-ply and radial-ply tyre are fitted on the same axle.
c   Both front tyres are under-inflated by 5 lbs per square inch.
d   The tyres are wider than the wheel arches of the car.

6   What would be the least amount of alcohol a driver could consume before the drink has any effect on driving performance or judgement?

a A pint of shandy (half beer and half lemonade).
b Two glasses of white wine with dinner.
c A double whisky taken with soda.
d Two pints of strong ale.

7   Which of the following is the only way in which a driver can cancel the effects of alcohol?

a Take lots of fresh air walking around the car park.
b Drink a glass of milk before taking in any alcohol.
c Allow at least one hour for every unit of alcohol.
d Eat a substantial meal whilst drinking.

8   If your vehicle is fitted with ABS braking what effect is this most likely to have on the vehicle and the way it can be driven?

a You can stop in a shorter distance.
b The brakes are better in the wet.
c You can steer and brake together.
d The front brakes will lock up quicker.

9   The national speed limit on dual-carriageway roads is

a 50 m.p.h.
b 60 m.p.h.
c 70 m.p.h.
d Dependent upon the weather conditions.

10   You are the first to arrive at the scene of a road-traffic accident on a rural road involving at least four or five cars. It is dark and raining. What should you do first?

a Telephone for the ambulance and fire brigade to arrive.
b Switch off any engines and warn oncoming traffic.
c Get the injured out of their cars to safety.
d Drive on to the next town to ring for help.

HOW WELL DID YOU DO?

Answers:

1 c You need to plan at least ten seconds ahead.
2 d Right of way does not exist on the roads.
3 c At ten car lengths you can see better and still change your mind.
4 b Long dry spells plus water create ideal skid-pan conditions.
5 a The minimum tyre tread depth is 1.6mm
6 a Any amount of alcohol has some effect on everyone.
7 c Time is the only way to disperse alcohol from the system.
8 c ABS prevents wheels locking; so you can steer and brake together.
9 c 70 m.p.h. is the national speed limit unless signed otherwise.
10 b Safeguard the scene first, avoid making the accident worse.

PERSONAL & VEHICLE INFORMATION DETAILS

Name: Driver No:
                                         Driving Licence expires: /   /
Address: Driving Licence Categories held:

Home Telephone: Daytime Telephone:

CAR INFORMATION RECORD

Make:	Model:	Reg No:

Important Details		
Local garage name:	Tel: Contact Name: Address:	
Breakdown Organization: Date expires: / /	Name: Tel: Emergency Tel:	
Motor insurance details (or broker if applicable): Telephone: Contact name:	Annual premium: £ Policy number: Name: Address: Comprehensive / Third Party Fire & Theft / Third Party Only	Date expires: / / Tel number:
MoT certificate:	Number:	Date expires: / /
Car registration:	Relicensing office:	Date expires: / /
Fuel:	Regular, Unleaded or Diesel:	Oil type:
Tyre pressures: Type and size:	Front: Rear:	
Mobile phone or emergency contact number:		

1 Going Places

Buying a car

What to do when you want to buy a new car (or second-hand car, new to you)

- Check first if it will fit your garage (or car-parking space).
- Appreciate the terms of the warranty or guarantee you get with it.
- Come to terms with payment – or make sure you can make the payments.
- Find out how much it will cost to insure – what group is it?
- Try all the seats for comfort.
- Check what safety features it has, and then what extras you may need or want in the future.

What to do when you've bought it

- Check the handbook.
- Check the spare wheel and tools.
- Check for any scratches or blemishes that weren't there before.
- Check that lights, electrics, wipers, washers, windows, etc. all work.
- Confirm the tax disc is valid, and MoT, if needed, is up to date.
- Check the insurance cover note is valid for you to drive.
- Check the invoice to show you have paid and have a receipt.
- Check the door locks, burglar alarm, and immobilizer are working (if not fitted, check to see if it would be worthwhile getting them).
- Make plans now for its first service and dummy MoT if needed.

The legal paperwork for car ownership

The Registration Document

You've passed your driving test. You've got yourself a car. You've got time off to go for a drive. What else do you need? Actually you need to know quite a lot more than your instructor told you. For instance, when you learned to drive you may have used the driving school or instructor's car. Although the driving examiner asked you if the test car was covered for insurance and you said yes, there is quite a lot more to know about car ownership and insurance. Let's start at the beginning.

Is it your own car? If so you should have the logbook – the Vehicle Registration Document – with your name and address on it. It is known by the DVLA, the Driver Vehicle Licensing Authority, at Swansea as a V5. If you don't have it, because you've only just bought the car, make sure you – and the previous owner – have sent the relevant details off straight away. If you have bought it new, the dealer will have done it for you. Failure to notify Swansea of any changes to ownership – or even of the colour – can result in a fine of up to £2,000.

However the form V5 does not prove you are the owner, it only says you are the registered keeper of the vehicle. Similarly, when you buy a car the fact that the person selling it has their name and address on the form is no genuine proof of ownership, and you need to know that it's not owned by a hire-purchase or leasing company. This is best done by a simple statement signed and witnessed stating that the seller has legal title to the car, and in exchange for so much money, is selling title of it to you. Any witness will do – as with any sale you are safer if you have a written contract which you can use in a court of law. So many cars are on hire purchase or leased, that if you do pay cash for a car which does not really belong to the seller, you can easily lose both the car and your cash if it is re-possessed. The DVLA also encourages vehicle owners (and keepers) of vehicles to register the present mileage of the car when it changes hands. The mileage is automatically recorded on the annual MOT certificates, but there is also space to include the mileage (voluntarily) on the registration document when you sell or buy a car. This is one way to keep an eye on those who try to make cars look younger – and thereby more expensive. It is not compulsory, but you need every help you can to know that the car you have just bought is as genuine as possible.

The MoT test certificate

If your car is more than three years old it will also need a certificate of road worthiness (called an MoT certificate). This is a legal requirement and this, with your licence and insurance certificate (not the policy, which is a huge document), is what you must show if you ever have to produce your 'driving documents' to a police officer. It is worthwhile keeping all these three available when you're driving. It saves having to take them to a police station within seven days, which is the alternative. Photocopies are not acceptable as proof of MoT, ownership or insurance as they can easily be altered and re-copied.

It is also worthwhile remembering that an MoT certificate does not say that a vehicle is actually roadworthy, just that it was at that particular time when it was tested. If you're buying an old car it's worth getting it tested immediately before you buy it. At least you will know more about the condition of it, and that it's safe at that particular time. Make sure there is an up-to-date MOT on the car. A genuine seller *will* be willing to pay the odd £20 to prove the car is roadworthy now. Or you could offer to pay if it passes provided the seller pays if it fails. An MoT more than three months old does not have this credibility. If you have any doubts about the validity of an MoT test certificate you can ring their hotline, 0891 615977, for help and advice.

If you've just bought a car which needs an MoT certificate, make sure that it's a fairly recent one. If it's more than 3 months old, you are sure that the seller would be happy to have it done again with a fresh 12 months starting from now. MoT car tests have been greatly strengthened over the past few years and now include a number of items which have never been tested before. Other items, such as exhaust emissions, now require considerably more effective testing and the percentage of hydrocarbons and other emissions allowed vary according to the age of the vehicle.

The items tested in the annual vehicle MoT test

Lighting: including headlamps, and that they are correctly aimed; stop lights, side and rear lights; rear reflectors; direction indicators and hazard lamps.

Steering and suspension: including steering control and mechanism; power steering; transmission shafts; wheel bearings; front and rear suspension; shock absorbers and wheel alignment.

Brakes: including any ABS and warning systems and control; condition of braking system; parking brake; brake performance; and any additional braking devices.

Tyres and wheels: tyre size and type; tyre load and speed ratings; tyre condition and wheels.

Seat belts: mountings, condition and operation.

General: Driver's view of the road; horn; exhaust system and emissions; general vehicle condition; mirrors; fuel system; registration plates and VIN numbers; speedo and any limiters; and other driving controls and glazing where applicable.

Insurance

Read every insurance proposal, policy, and certificate you get with great care. Find out exactly what you are covered for, and make sure you know what you cannot claim for. If the other driver is to blame you still need to inform your own insurers; but put the words 'without prejudice' at the beginning of the letter. This helps to safeguard your policy from any claim on it. There are a variety of insurance options you can choose.

Comprehensive
This is probably the best known: it means that as well as the Third Party, Fire, and Theft terms (see below) in the event of an accident you will be able to claim for the repairs to your own vehicle on your insurance. If the fault of the accident was another motorist or vehicle driver's, and you can get them to agree to it, then their insurers will pay for your damage and costs, but you must always read the small print of your insurance certificate to be certain.

Third Party, Fire, and Theft
If your car is a bit older – say ten years or so – you may find that you are limited by your insurers to Third Party, Fire, and Theft coverage only. 'Third Party' refers to accidents: the insurance company is the party of the first part of the agreement; you, the insured, are the party of the second part; anyone else who gets involved becomes the party of the third part. Third Party insurance cover will pay the costs that may arise as a result of your actions to any person, whether it is for injury or damage to their property. If you reverse into someone's fence your insurance cover should pay for the damage. If you accidentally open your door as a cyclist passes and the poor unfortunate cyclist falls under a steamroller your

insurance should cover the costs involved, which may include any potential earnings that his widow could have expected from him for the next few years. The highest insurance claim I ever came across personally was a driving instructor who accidentally reversed into an electrical sub-station and cost his insurance company over a quarter of a million pounds. But I also heard about the Frenchman in his little 2CV who stalled on a level crossing, then derailed a train carrying chemicals which spilled into a city's water supply. The cost of that made the French national debt look like pocket money. His annual premium was less than £43 and was for third party only.

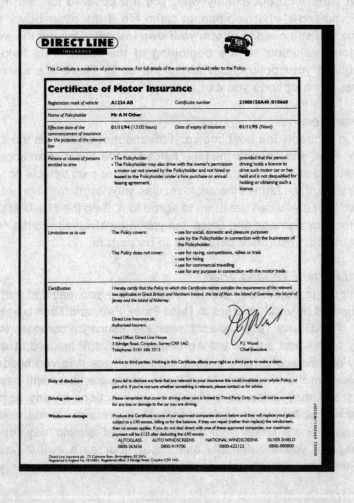

Third Party only or – as it is known – Legal Cover only, is the minimum insurance cover you can have. This means that if you damage or hurt any third party or passenger in any accident they can still claim against your insurance if you are at fault. The important thing to note about this minimum cover is that your car is not covered for damage and the driver, whether it is you or anyone else, is not covered for injury. Incidentally in some instances, such as where a cyclist or pedestrian is involved, your insurance company may have to pay for an ambulance call out, simply because you were involved in, or at the scene of, a road-traffic accident. It may not have been your fault, but your insurance still pays out. And you can lose your no-claims bonus too.

> **Third party insurance cover is essential.** *Never* **drive uninsured, even for a short journey. It's illegal and even if you can afford the penalty points, plus the potential of a huge fine or imprisonment, third party costs could easily bankrupt you.**

> *Legal Cover only*
> **If you can't afford Third Party, Fire and Theft, you must opt for minimal Legal Cover, or Third Party only. Never risk driving, or allow anyone to drive your car, uninsured.**

The premium and the no-claims bonus

The initial premium, or amount you are asked to pay, can soon be reduced to less than a third provided you can maintain a series of two or three years without any claims. This produces what every driver knows as a no-claims bonus of up to 60 or 70%. Unfortunately many drivers think of it as a no-blame bonus, and this it is not. If you make a claim and the insurance company have to pay out on your behalf, you can't expect them to reduce your premium next year.

There are three ways to safeguard your NCB potential. The most obvious one is to avoid getting into an accident – and claim – situation. Follow the advice in this book and you shouldn't have one. The second is to protect your NCB by paying an additional premium.

Ask your insurers if you can do this. Some of them will let you, some want you to, and others might be persuaded to let you.

The third is to carry what is known as a 'voluntary excess'. If you are a new driver, a young driver, or have a bad record, you won't have a great deal of choice. The insurance company will probably insist that you pay the first £30, £50, or more of any claim. This is the excess. You can better that by offering to pay the first £100 or even £200 instead. This will reduce your initial premium considerably, and also make you a bit more reluctant to have an accident or a claim.

The car and the garage

Selecting the right fuel and filling up properly

The one place which can almost guarantee to get rid of that great feeling of elation you got when you passed your driving test is just round the corner. It happens the first time you have to fill up your car – especially when it's your very own car – with fuel. Note the use of the word 'fuel' and not petrol; even if your car needs petrol and not diesel, there are still too many pumps looming up at you. Do you need unleaded, super unleaded, or premium? Even more worrying, do you know where the fuel goes into your tank and can you open it? Many cars have locking fuel caps, and unless you know how some of them can be difficult to open. Some car manufacturers, especially a few years ago, seemed to take great pride in hiding the fuel cap behind the number plate. Even now, in the interests of smooth lines, most vehicles have their fuel cap hidden inside the rear wing and you need to know where the latch is and how to open it. The fuel cap itself often locks and may require a special knack and/or a key to open it. Remember to replace the cap afterwards.

Your car is	Your fuel pump is	Your fuel is	Meant for
Diesel	Black	Diesel	Diesel-engined vehicles only
Registered D or before	Red	Four-star (premium) leaded	Older cars without catalytic converters
Registered E or F	Red / Green	Four-star / Unleaded	
Registered G or later	Green (probably)	Unleaded	
	Green	Unleaded	
Registered J or later	Yellow and green stripes	Extra-clean unleaded	For cars with catalytic converters
	Blue	Super unleaded	

Cars with an F or G registration were the first to use 'unleaded' fuel as standard. Cars registered L or later are normally fitted with catalysers (catalytic converters) which means that they mustn't use leaded fuel and you can destroy them by push starting or bump starting the car. 'Unburned' fuel goes through an engine if the sparking plugs do not ignite it and the explosive mixture goes through to the exhaust system. (This is what happens when you push start a car; the first few cylinders of movement do not ignite.) This fuel can easily destroy the delicate composition of a catalytic converter so if a new one is needed it can prove to be an expensive push start.

Cars older than E or F will amost certainly need Four Star (Premium) leaded petrol. Don't put unleaded fuel in, as it will eventually damage the engine.

If your car uses **diesel**, don't put petrol in.

Fuel Pump Colour Codes

Black = Diesel
Blue   = Super Unleaded
Green = Unleaded
Red   = Leaded
Yellow and Green Stripes mean 'Extra clean unleaded fuel'

Check before you fill up

When you've made sure you're at the correct pump, lift the nozzle off the pump and make sure the readings go back to zero. Push the nozzle as far into your tank as you can. If it won't go in confirm that it is the right nozzle for your car: four-star hoses have larger nozzles than unleaded ones. Press the trigger and keep it pressed until the meter reads the amount you want to pay or until the pump stops automatically. Fuel cut-offs prevent you washing your car, tyres, and the forecourt with petrol; and they are usually very efficient. This is one reason why it's worthwhile always using the same garage. Once you've found a good, efficient, and cheap garage near to you, it is well to keep using it for most of your fuel needs. Once they get to know you, they might allow you credit whilst you go back home to fetch your wallet.

Make sure you have the means to pay for the fuel before you start to fill your tank; it can be embarrassing to see them siphon it out again.

Other forecourt facilities
By using the same garage or fuel supplier you can quickly learn how to use their other forecourt facilities too. Most garages provide free water and air for your screen washer, windscreen, and tyres. Tyres, screen washers, oil levels, and other fluids need to be checked at least once a week, sometimes daily if you cover a lot of miles. If you set aside a regular time and place for these checks, it easily becomes a comfortable and sensible habit. The comfort factor comes from knowing that you will never be taken by surprise with an empty screen washer halfway through a long motorway journey with trucks spraying your windscreen every time your paths cross. It is illegal to drive with a dirty windscreen or an empty screen-wash container, so work out how often you need to fill it up and know where you can get water for it. Ideally you should do this at leisure at home, but if this isn't convenient, then use your local garage instead. Don't put anti-freeze in the screen-washer bottle, it will damage the paintwork, but add some form of proprietory screen cleaner to help get rid of grease and insects.

You need to check your oil level before you have driven, when the engine is cold. Tyre pressures too must be checked when the tyres are cold.

When you check them, look and feel for other things: run your hands lightly around the surface for anything stuck into the treads, and feel and look for bulges, cuts, and anything else which could cause you grief later on. If you do have to change a wheel, far better to do it at home or on a garage forecourt before you leave than at night in the rain on a country lane.

Passengers in your car

As the proud owner of a new (to you) car, you will never be short of passengers. Friends, friends of friends, and your family will all be keen to take a ride with you — once you have got over the first few drives on your own. The law does have a few things to say about passengers, and you the driver are involved as well.

All children under the age of fourteen must wear seat belts where they are fitted, or be in child seats, booster cushions or similar child safety harnesses. This is your legal responsibility, and if you are faced with children who don't want to wear belts, or prefer to run wild on the back seat, you are allowed to hit them with a rolled-up copy of the Highway Code to impress on them your legal position. Make sure that your car takes the best child seats, and that they can be fitted properly. Not all modern cars will take them. Rear-facing seats are best for very young children, and if you are driving alone with them fit these to the front passenger seat so you can see them clearly. If you have children in the back, rather than keep turning round to look at them while you're running into the back of a bus, it's better to fix a second mirror like your driving instructor used, so you can keep them in view and still drive safely. If your car is fitted with air bags you must not use rear facing children's seats in the front. It can be dangerous for them. All children's seats are best fitted by an expert – someone who knows how that particular seat must be fitted. Don't just hope that the seat belt will keep it in place.

Passengers over the age of fourteen are also required to wear seat belts, in the back seats and in the front, where belts are fitted. The only difference from your point of view is that they face – and have to pay – the fine if they don't. You have two answers to any suggestions from your passengers that they needn't bother. If they don't wear seat belts in your car they don't travel. And you can add that survivors will be prosecuted and can be fined on the spot. You could always threaten to collect the £50 fine per person from them, in advance, per journey, and then donate it to charity.

The only answer is that all passengers must stay belted up whilst you are driving.

Keeping your car

A clean car not only looks good, it holds its value too. Clean it once a week; and if you are even the slightest bit lazy about it, you can put it through a car wash first for about a pound or so. That way the machine takes all the serious dirt and grime off, and you can clean it properly yourself at your leisure. Car washes are not expensive, but it is even cheaper (and you certainly get a better result) to give the car a really good scrub, inside and out, and remove every bit of grime from paintwork and glass, every now and again. Don't forget to close your window once you have pressed the start button!

Daily, weekly and monthly car checks

Daily
- Fuel   Confirm you have enough to start your journey.
- Electrics   That all lights and bulbs are working.
- Tyres   Check for bulges or apparent pressure loss.
- Windscreen   Clean and clear, with no obstructions.
- Horn   Moving test – but avoid annoyance.

Weekly
- Oil   Use the dipstick to test level and viscosity.
- Radiator   Check coolant level – check when cold.
- Battery   Electrolyte level and clean terminals.
- Fluids   Check clutch and brake fluid levels.
- Tyres   Treads, pressures, bulges and cuts.
- Steering wheel   Excessive play or noises.

Monthly
- Oil filter   Check against mileage and service needs.
- Air filter   Remove and shake, if suitable put back.
- Drive belts   Check for proper tensioning.
- Wheels   Check tracking and change round if needed.

Each winter and summer check for anti-freeze, de-icer in screen wash, and position of air intake if it needs to be seasonally adjusted.

Read and study your car handbook with regard to the various routine safety checks. Or get the local garage to do it for you the first time, whilst you watch. Then you'll see what an easy habit it is to get into to check your car for safety's sake, every day, every week, and every month.

Finally, if you have bought a brand-new car, or if it's leased to you, then you really need to ensure that it is checked, serviced, and looked after by the garage where you bought it. But if it's an older car, possibly one that was quite expensive when new, it's not always economical to take it back to the original garage for servicing and spares. Quite often the little man round the corner can do as good a job as the big garage. He is probably more efficient, will treat you like a valued customer, and be prepared to look after your car more cheaply than the original dealer would. To him you are a good customer; to a bigger dealer you are not. Remember he is in the business of looking after his customers, whereas most of the bigger garages are mainly in the business of selling cars and making money.

Points to remember

- Check the ownership of a vehicle you are buying, as well as its history.
- Make sure you inform DVLA about the change of ownership.
- Shop around for the best insurance policy for you.
- Aim to get into a no-claims bonus situation as soon as you can.
- Keep your driving documents with you in the car.
- Find out what fuel your car uses, and how to fill it up.
- Check your tyre pressures when cold, each week, and look for cuts, foreign objects, or wear and tear on the tread.
- Check your screen-wash bottle is full, and use water or a proper screen-wash fluid (not washing-up liquid, which tends to smear).
- Keep track of your fuel costs in pence per mile; sudden increased costs can become more expensive if you don't find out the cause.
- Build up a relationship with your local garage, you might need to rely on their help one day.
- Keep your car clean, safe, legal, and working efficiently. Make it keep its value, for you will need the best price for it when you get your next new car.

YOUR TOOL-KIT

Over the years you will probably build up a comprehensive tool-kit to keep in the car. With most drivers this kit is made up from the hard lesson of experience, caused by a realization of 'I wish I had it with me now.'

Here is a list of the sort of tools, pieces of equipment, and items which may get you out of a jam. No doubt in three years' time you will have added to this list too.

- Basic wheel-change kit. This is normally supplied, but check it now!
- A decent jack. Those supplied rarely are!
- A long or extended wheel brace. You can buy these in most car shops, but they take the effort out of removing wheel nuts.
- A set of jump leads. These are thick copper leads with grips on the ends to connect two batteries together when you can't start your car.
- A decent sized tow rope. Get one with good fixings so that you can connect them easily to each car. Don't tie them round your bumper though. All modern cars are fitted with 'towing eyes' built in, under the front and rear bumpers. These are metal circles about two inches in diameter, large enough to thread a rope or hook through. They are normally used to hold vehicles down when they are stacked six or more at a time on transporter lorries and are strong enough for an occasional tow provided not too much weight is suddenly pulled on them.
- A piece of old carpet or sacking, and a shovel. You won't need these in the summer, but if you drive in snow or ice, you'll be glad you have them.
- A good hand-lamp. You can buy them for multi-purpose use, some have hazard lights which flash independently of the main beam.
- A rug or heavy coat. A rug can cover the back seat and take up no space, but if you break down in the winter you will be glad of the extra warmth.
- Maps and guide books. A good UK atlas is quite cheap, but it is always worth having a few extra large-scale maps of areas you visit frequently.
- A clean duster, sponge, and window leather. Keeping windows clean is always easier if you keep the cleaning material in a separate plastic bag.
- Ice scraper and de-icer fluid. These are only essential in the winter months, but make sure you put them back in before the bad weather starts.
- Some screen-washer fluid. This is useful at any time when you top up the washer bottle, or to clean the windscreen from summer flies.
- A spare key. Don't hide the spare key where a thief can find it. But if you can locate it securely somewhere safe, you may save yourself from embarrassment.
- Pliers. Three pairs, with different types of grip, are all you need. Large and heavy, side cutters for wires, and a pair of long-nosed ones.
- Spanners. A cheap set is all you need, but make sure they fit your vehicle. The usual sizes are metric, and are shown as 10 mm to 20 mm, etc.
- Screwdrivers. You need a variety, ranging from small electrical ones to a heavy one which you can use as a lever in an emergency.
- Spare bulbs and fuses. Find out what sort your car needs and collect a few of the more important ones.
- Oddments of string, sticky tape, and lengths of wire. These really depend on your own ingenuity and abilities.
- Warning triangle. This is essential for breakdowns, and a legal requirement in many countries.
- First-aid kit. It is best to get a really good one. The small ones don't really have much in them. Have a good set and take some training to match.

Keep as much of the kit as you can in a small bag or box. Although this list looks long and detailed, most of the items will be accumulated over a period of time.

CHANGING A WHEEL

Very few drivers actually change a wheel before the circumstances are forced upon them. Unfortunately this is often when it's too late to learn.

1 Find the safest place to carry out the exercise.
   Ensure the brakes are on and wheels chocked. Put the gear lever in first or reverse. Get out your spare wheel and tools and lay them out. Put the new wheel under the body near the jacking point. Remove the hub cap (if necessary with a screwdriver).

2 Use the wheel brace to loosen the wheel nuts first. If they are locked, use as long a lever on your wheel brace as possible, and stand on it to get the first movement started.

3 Jack up the body: make sure it's high enough to get the new wheel on. Continue to loosen the wheel nuts. Remove them and place them in the hub cap.

4 Remove the wheel. Replace it with the spare and put the old wheel under the body. Check that the bevelled side of the nuts faces into the wheel. Put each wheel nut on and finger tighten them, then use the brace to tighten each of them in turn.

5 Slowly release the jack, and then tighten up the nuts as much as you can.

6 Replace the hub cap, collect the spare wheel and pack it away for replacement (likely) or repair (very unlikely, if you have had a puncture you really need a new tyre). Collect up and put away all your tools.

AVOID
- Changing a wheel at night, in the dark, with your body in the road.
- Reaching or groping under the car body when it is jacked up.
- Changing a wheel on a motorway at any time on the driver's side.
- Changing a wheel if you are parked on a hill.

ALWAYS
- Get some practice beforehand.
- Know the proper sequence before you even start.
- Change a wheel on the level.
- Make sure your parking brake is on, and all wheels are chocked.
- Keep an old jacket and gloves handy in the car.

2 Town Driving

Everyday driving is one of the reasons why most people take their driving test. They want a driving licence so they are no longer dependent upon other people, buses, cycling, or walking to get around. Buses are not the best way to shop; and certainly not the best way to get your shopping home again. And it is frustrating for all parties to keep asking other people to give you lifts everywhere. Especially when they refuse. Now that you've passed your test and have your own car, you'll soon find how awkward it is when everyone else wants to use you as the community taxi.

Nevertheless you've got to start on your own somewhere, and now that you have your licence, and a car, properly insured and full of fuel, what else do you need? The answer is a system. To start with you can forget some of the heavy advice which has been thrown at you since you started your driving lessons. Such things as 'don't cross your hands or you'll fail your test', never were true; but now you need to drive for yourself and not to please an examiner. The only people you have to please now are all the other road users you'll meet, any policemen, magistrates, your insurance company, and people who might bend your car if you put it in the wrong place.

Let's start from the beginning.

Before you drive off

Drivers' attitudes and road safety
Remember to switch on your good driving attitude before you start. It is not enough to be healthy and physically fit. If you wake up in a bit of a mood, or have a row with someone, don't take it into the car with

you. A good driving attitude will get you to your destination and back home again safely. A bad one could lead to a total disaster.

There are four separate aspects to your driving attitude: your responsibility to other road users; your commitment to caring for their safety; showing courtesy and consideration to all of them all the time; your pride in driving as safely and carefully as you can always. You need to check your car – of course, but you must also check yourself! Are you fit to drive? It's not just a question of being sober, having no declared illnesses, drugs, or disabilities. You have to be in the right frame of mind. Even something like a slight headache means you must take extra care. *One degree under – 5 m.p.h. slower! Three degrees under – don't drive.*

What you need to remember before moving off – every time

F   Fuel – petrol or diesel, is there enough to get you there?
L   Look – all round, make sure all the windows are clean and clear.
O   Oil – somewhere between the maximum and minimum marks.
W   Water – not only the radiator, check the washer bottle too.
E   Electrics – check your lights, indicators, and brake lights.
R   Rubber – tyres, wiper blades, and hoses all legal and safe.
Y   Yourself – are you (the nut behind the wheel) in a fit state to drive?

This is one system which will stand you in good stead. There are various mnemonics to help you to remember the various safety checks. FLOWERY is as good as any. Think of it as a personal security check before you drive off anywhere, and you'll not come unstuck through lack of fuel, or no water in the washer bottle, or losing your grip in the wet. There are many variations on the same theme of course and if your instructor gave you one you can remember easily, then use that. If not, then remember to check FLOWERY every day before you move off.

There are further vehicle safety and moving-off checks, of course. You will have learned these as part of your early driving lessons. Nevertheless it is worth repeating them, just in case you have become forgetful now that the driving examiner is not in your thoughts.

Cockpit drill
Is it safe to open the door before you get in?
Get in quickly, but safely. Close the door properly. Close all the

doors properly. Remember all the doors and your passengers are your concern now. Listen for the double click which ensures the doors are properly closed.

This leads on to the other checks which you may remember from your driving lessons.

D Treble S M

You may have your own variation on this. But if not, this one is as good as any, and better than most because it covers all your needs.

Close all **D**oors;
check that your **S**eat is comfortable and
that you can reach the **S**teering wheel properly.
Ensure everyone is wearing their **S**eat belt correctly.
Finally make sure you can see through each of the **M**irrors.

Remember to adjust the passenger door mirror too. Some driving instructors make a habit of using the left door one themselves and not all learner drivers are used to them. Proper and constant use of this door mirror is a life-saver, and can save you from embarrass- ment, and perhaps a cyclist, one day. The time to adjust your mirrors is before you start to move off, not when you are halfway down the road. If necessary get someone to walk round the car for you whilst you adjust each mirror in turn to suit your own personal comfort and needs.

Carry out a few new extra checks too

Make sure the parking brake is on, and try your brakes for a static brake test. Press the clutch right down as well. If someone else may have driven it since you last sat in it, check that your seat is really in the position you feel most comfortable. If the car is strange to you, find out where all the various switches and other controls are. Take special care to confirm where the indicator switch is placed. The hallmark of the novice driver in a strange car is putting the wipers on every time they want to turn. Try the steering wheel too, for any extra slackness.

Starting drill

Always make sure that the parking brake is firmly applied and that the gear lever is in neutral before you turn the key in the ignition. Don't check it the other way round or you may find yourself rolling down the hill. When you have finished with the car, leave it that way too. If it's not your car and the owner insists you keep it in gear to stop it rolling down hills when parked, ask if you can have the brakes checked before you drive it again. Note the words 'parking brake'. Not all parking brakes are hand operated.

Switched on
Warning lights on; ignition switched on. Turn the key and hear the engine start first or second time. The warning lights should all go off except for brake warning light and the choke if there is one. Is there? While you are looking, also see what other warning lights come on and then go off. Do you know what they all mean? Check with your vehicle's handbook to see what you should do if any of them stay on when they shouldn't.

Fuel check
Once the engine has been turned on, you should check your fuel level. Never drive far on a nearly empty tank and avoid driving on sludge from the bottom of the fuel tank. It can cause your engine to stop and it can be quite expensive to clean the tank out.

Brake test
Although you carry out a static brake test when you do your cockpit drill, try your brake lights as soon as you can if there is a convenient car, window, or wall behind you, or ask someone to tell you. Make sure you carry out a running brake test very soon after you have started. It need not be a severe one; just hard enough to know that they won't let you down. As always with these checks what you are looking for is any change from previous occasions. This is also why it is useful to let someone else try your brakes occasionally too.

Know where you are going
One of the worst feelings is moving off without knowing where you are going. So on your early runs, and especially when you are going somewhere new or strange, take time to read a map, and plan out a route before you actually get in the car.

   If the car is OK, everyone is ready, and you know where you're going, off you go.

Your first trip alone

Try to choose a journey with some degree of excitement – but not fear – in it. Perhaps you could drive around the area where you've been having your lessons, and then take a right turn out into the country. Depending upon your own personality, you may prefer to stick to the route you have planned and pored over beforehand, or you may choose to keep following the road ahead until you are well and truly in another world.

Try not to make it the next one, though. Remember you must still plan your driving even if you haven't planned your route.

What if it all goes wrong?
If you find yourself going the wrong way, don't worry. It won't be difficult to find your way back. And if you have allowed yourself plenty of time, no one need ever know you went off track. If you get desperate don't abandon the car in some strange high street or country lane, wait until you find a convenient parking spot, off the road, if you can, then find out where you are, and how you can get back to where you want to go. If you get really lost, ask a responsible-looking person – a policeman, traffic warden, or shop-keeper is the best choice. If you are a young and frightened female it is best not to ask the first aggressive-looking male for help. If you are a young, aggressive male, you'd probably be too scared to ask a young, pretty, and frightened-looking female too.

Maps and street plans
Always keep a national atlas and larger scale maps of the district where you live in the car. Even a car phone – for emergency use only – can be a sensible investment.

Safe driving in the town

One thing that will make you feel happy is to discover that the same rules you learned whilst you were learning to drive apply just the same when you are on your own. I am sure you will remember them well. *Mirror – Signal – Mirror* works every time. The second phase,

Position – Speed – Look, works just as well, and fits in with the third phase, *Look – Assess – Decide*.

However, you are a competent driver – at least, the driving examiner was convinced that you were competent, and experience will only come with time. So you might like to try a new road sequence, which is exactly the same as MSM, PSL and LAD, but is easier to think about. The three things to control – in sequence – every time you make a decision are *Position – Speed – Gear* with the very important addition of making use of *Full Observation* all the time to ensure that information is both received and given when needed. The idea is to separate the mechanical movements of steering, braking, accelerating, and gear changing from the important mental approach of being fully aware of everyone else on the road, and being prepared to tell them what you are going to do.

Full Observation and Information in and out		
Position then **Speed** then **Gears**		

This is exactly the same as MSM, PSL, and LAD, but it puts it into better perspective. Let your eyes and brain concentrate on the need to see what is happening and to tell everyone else what you are doing, and at the same time allow your muscles and bones to concentrate on the physical tasks of getting the car into the correct position, adjusting the speed to suit the road and traffic conditions, and selecting the correct gear for the next action you intend to take.

The real driving skills

Looking all around you takes on a new meaning when you are driving completely on your own. First of all you need to know who to make eye contact with, and how to do so. Then you need to build up your assessment and anticipation skills. We all need good perception skills and a logical but keen imagination in order to assist in the new decision-making processes that you will need from now on, whenever you are in the car.

Driving no longer consists of just the gear changes and clutch control sequences of your learning days. Instead you need to develop very good *visual search skills* and *decision-making skills*. These are the real driving skills.

Observation and information

Too many drivers assume that once they've looked in their mirrors and given a signal the world is theirs to do as they wish. The truth is that you need to keep your eyes and ears constantly looking and listening for everything around you, filtering out everything that doesn't or won't concern you, and telling everyone who needs it what you intend to do. Then do it as positively and smoothly as you can. You will find now your driving lessons are finished that all of the physical things you struggled so hard to remember and master when you were learning have become automatic reactions.

Use your own autopilot

When you first started to drive every gear change was a momentous occasion. Now you can scarcely remember whether you changed gear or not. It just happens. The conscious part of the brain is no longer concerned with the mechanical aspects of driving. The practical elements of driving become a matter of instinct and are almost intuitive. This is the stage of competence required by a driving examiner to allow someone to drive on their own. However this does not mean you can go to sleep at the wheel. Some things still need to be thought about. Things like watching out for other road users, and obeying all traffic signs and warnings.

Competence leads to proficiency

You cannot rely on anyone else to tell you when to brake or speed up. All driving decisions, as opposed to mechanical ones, still need conscious thought and action. This is what the driving examiner looked for, and in your case found acceptable. This competence stage is only part way to becoming an expert. In between you will need to become proficient. Proficiency is part of the way to becoming an expert.

Proficiency leads to expertise

This is the beginning of successful driving on your own. For example, you may feel the need to sound the horn on an odd occasion or two. This is probably something you would rarely, if ever, have been allowed to do in your driving lessons. Now you are on your own, occasions will arise (not very often, but you never know in advance), when you need to give information to another road user who can't see you, but might need to be told you are around. If the horn is needed, use it. However use it only for information that you are there, and not as a rebuke or challenge to anyone else. Certainly avoid using it if anyone, especially if it's not intended for them, might take umbrage. If you hear a horn sound, it makes you feel guilty. Don't make others feel it too. As you become proficient you will know when and how to use all your controls – not only those on the vehicle, but also the control you have over other road users. Use them sparingly, but to the maximum effect. This is where proficiency begins to lead to expertise. A proficient driver is one who can make good use of the road and vehicle. An expert driver is one who does it all smoothly without apparent effort and without upsetting anyone else.

Driving on autopilot

Driving on 'autopilot' means proficiency. It is a state you will very soon achieve, but until you reach it, one that seems almost impossible to accept. Nevertheless, although 'autopilot' driving is a happy state to be in, it always requires extreme concentration on the mental activities involved in driving. You must always use your mirrors consciously. You should always give a signal, whether by arm, indicator, or horn, as a deliberate act to inform other road users what you are doing. The moment you rely on instinct or habit to give or receive information, you will find yourself in trouble.

Thinking driving – a step towards advanced driving

Driving automatically means thinking about what you need to do, but not about how you do it. This allows you to concentrate your efforts on looking, on hazard perception, classification, and avoidance, and planning the safest route through the road and traffic minefields.

Decision making in town traffic

On long runs you can make your own decisions where and when to stop. In town your decisions are often made for you. Traffic lights and stop and give way signs all tell you who has priority and when it is your turn to go. During your lessons you will have become used to stopping for traffic lights and at pedestrian crossings. Now you need to plan your driving to take advantage of traffic controllers to keep your driving as smooth as possible.

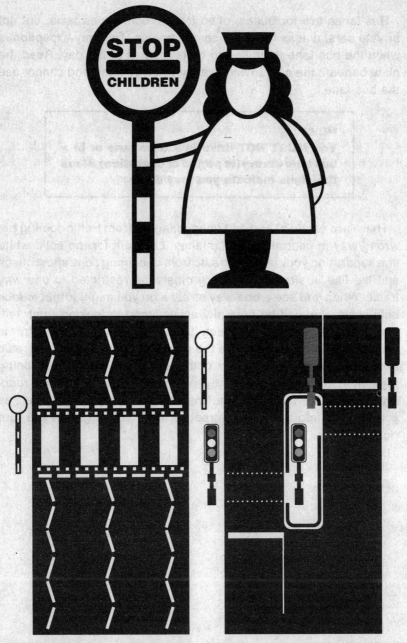

Treat crossings as if they were pieces of pavement and encourage pedestrians to use them – but not by waving them across. If a crossing has a 'refuge' in the middle of the road (see illustration bottom right), consider it as two separate crossings.

Bus lanes are for buses, often cycles, sometimes taxis, but not private cars, unless the signs say otherwise. The only exception is when the bus lane is limited to certain times of the day. Read the plate beneath the sign to see exactly when you can and cannot use the bus lane.

HC 97
You MUST NOT drive in a tram lane or in a bus lane during its period of operation unless the signs indicate you may do so.

There are especial and additional dangers from traffic coming the wrong way in contraflow traffic lanes. Look out for the solid white line separating your lanes of traffic from oncoming contraflow buses and the like in streets which are otherwise restricted to one way traffic. When you see a one-way street sign you might forget to look both ways. You will be normally accustomed to looking right, left, and right again as you approach junctions, and in one-way streets you may be tempted to ignore the potential of any oncoming traffic from the wrong direction. In both cases you must avoid being frightened by traffic apparently on the wrong side of the road. Always assume that someone may be coming from your left as you turn left into a one-way street, or from your right as you turn right into one.

> **Parking guide:**
> **It is always easier to reverse into a parking**
> **bay at the kerb than to drive in frontwards.**

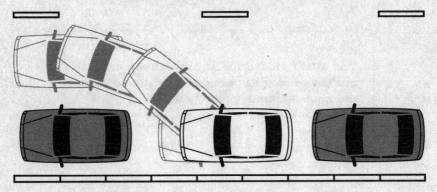

Parking in reverse gear is easier – when you are confident.

Points to remember

- Improve your observation skills.
- Make proper judgement of other road users and their actions.
- Be more aware of what is happening around you.
- Make proper use of eye contact with other road users.
- Look out for vulnerable road users, especially for the old, young, and infirm.
- Make adequate allowance for pedestrians crossing the road, even where crossing is not allowed.
- Approach pedestrian crossings safely and be able to stop with consideration.
- Reduce speed when children are around – even if they seem safe enough.
- Avoid following too close to vehicles ahead.
- Turn right safely, and with a sure guarantee that you can complete the turn safely.
- Overtake with great care, knowing you can get past safely.
- Be aware of your limited fields of vision.
- Know how to cope with all kinds of road junctions and traffic management systems.
- FINALLY: Know that you must always create and maintain your own safety cushion around you.

3 Out of Town Driving

When you are driving away from the discipline of town roads, the pace of life changes. Your speed is no longer controlled by the traffic ahead and around you, and the amount of control exerted on you by the local authorities is reduced, so you won't have as many traffic lights, give way signs, and other traffic controllers. But there are still all the normal road disciplines to bear in mind, and since you may drive on the same road for twenty or thirty miles without reaching a single junction, your own hazard-perception skills and decision-making skills become much more important.

Your progress depends entirely upon yourself and what you want to do. The first time you venture out of the town and into the country in your own car, you may simply want to enjoy the freedom of going where you want without anyone else telling you what to do. You can choose your own speed and which direction you take. You can even choose whether to get out the map, plan your journey in meticulous detail, and follow it precisely, or just follow your car's bonnet and see where you end up.

Your first long journey

Plan a proper timetable for that first long exciting trip, and if it is likely to last more than two hours make sure you allow for breaks, or what are coyly called 'comfort stops'. If your route involves motorways make sure you know before you start off where you can pull in at service stations on the way. Until the end of 1994 it was possible to join the motorway at Dover in Kent, drive over two hundred miles, following the M20, M2, M26, M25, M40, M42 and finally the M5 before you eventually came across the first service station just south of

Birmingham. No wonder visitors from the Continent considered the British to be a strange race. Dover may well be the gateway to the Continent; but for visitors to Britain, our motorway network is not always the best place for the incontinent.

The situation has improved considerably, but you still need to know where suitable service stations are, in order to take advantage of them. Remember too that fuel prices, like food prices, on motor-ways are exorbitant, and it often makes sense to get off the motorway to refuel both the car and the passengers. On the other hand, if you plan your fuel stops well, it makes sense to give yourself a physical break – getting out of the car and walking for a while – at least every two hours. Even experienced drivers need this. If this is your first long drive, take a break every hour or so. Even when you have lots of experience you still will benefit from stopping for a physical break. Two hours is the longest you should ever drive without a break. Even if your body doesn't want a comfort stop your brain needs a rest.

Reading the road

Whichever way you choose, you still have to follow one simple rule. Read the road, and allow your speed and position to be controlled by what you see. Reading the road means looking and anticipating what may be round the next bend at any time. Expect a tractor or a combine harvester; if you are lucky it may only be a herd of cows. Reading the road gives you time to plan each move you make. Once you have hit the open road and left the town's speed limits behind you can allow your speed to increase as close to 60 m.p.h. (provided you are subject to the national speed limit for single-carriageway roads) as your fancy and the road and traffic conditions allow. Now you have achieved the degree of competence required by a driving examiner your brain tells your limbs to maintain a set speed in a correct position and the rest is done through 'auto pilot'.

The first things to note are about the road ahead of you. Ask yourself a series of questions about it.

● How wide is it?
● What sort of surface does it have?
● Is there an obvious camber away from the centre?

- Does the camber only go one way?
- Is the road straight?
- What might be round the corner?
- How much traffic is on it?

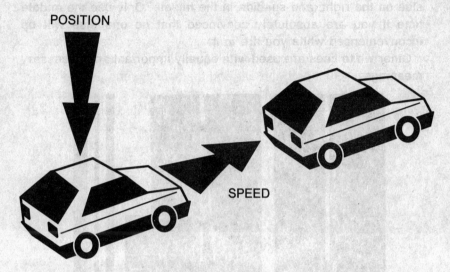

POSITION

SPEED

Always be aware of your speed and position in relation to other road users. The position is controlled by the steering and the speed is controlled by the accelerator and brake.

Road markings

Next study any white lines painted at the centre or the edges of the road. They will tell you quite a lot about the road itself. The centre line indicates your part of the road. You should not cross this line unless you need to and it is safe. If the road is very narrow then you may be forced to straddle the centre line in order to maintain your correct position. In this case you will need to look for passing places. You may even have to reverse into one.

Remember that two facing cars cannot both straddle the centre line. If there is any doubt, you must get in as close to the left as possible and slow down to let the oncoming traffic get by. If you are still not sure, stop. However most rural roads will have at least two lanes, and occasionally three.

1 Double white lines

If you're driving on a three-lane single carriageway, you often find that one direction of traffic has priority. This is indicated by the double white line system, using a solid line and a broken line. Priority is given to the traffic which has the broken line their side (A). There is only one thing to remember about three-lane single carriageways. The three lanes indicate: our side on the left; their side on the right; and sui-cide in the middle. Only use the middle lane if you are absolutely convinced that no one else will be inconvenienced while you are in it.

Other white lines are used with equally important and necessary meanings.

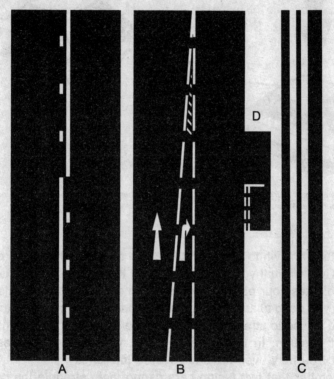

Read the white lines on the road as you would read any road sign.

2 Short broken lines with long gaps
These show the centre; but if the amount of paint increases, it means look out for danger.

3 Single broken lines with long markings and short gaps along the centre of the road (B)
These show that a hazard exists. See if you can identify the hazard

now. A hazard can be anything. This is where your hazard perception and avoidance skills come to the fore. Plan your driving so that you always have an option. Most decisions are simple ones: stop or go. Stop may not always be the safest one, but it's safer than go if you're not sure. The secret of decision making is that it's not always which one you choose, but making your decision at the right time.

4   Short broken white lines divide the road into lanes

If the council see fit to paint white lines you shouldn't go round rubbing them out. Stay in your lane.

5   Solid white lines or broken lines at the edge of the road on country lanes

These make drivers aware of where the side of the road is at night or in conditions of bad visibility. Solid lines are used to show that the road bends more than if the lines are broken.

6   Double white lines down the centre of any road (C)

You must not cross these lines or straddle them if the solid line is on your side unless there are special circumstances. As a new driver you may even know the new rules regarding crossing these lines better than older experienced drivers. You can cross them if you need access to premises on the right, or if you need to pass a stationary obstruction. The new rules allow you to overtake (and cross the lines) to get past pedal cycles, horses being ridden or led, and road-maintenance vehicles travelling at less than 10 m.p.h. Ask any other experienced drivers you know if they are aware of these changes.

Where a centre double line widens and is filled with white diagonal stripes it is used to reinforce the need to avoid crossing it (D). If the outside lines are both solid, then the diagonal hatch markings form part of a double white line system and must not be crossed or entered. If the outer lines are broken, then you should only cross them if it is essential to your safe driving progress.

Road signs

Red means prohibitory; blue is mandatory.
Both must be obeyed.

*A red circle containing a black bicycle means **no cycling**, but
a blue circle with a white bicycle means **for cyclists only**.*

Circular signs give commands, triangular ones are warnings.

Road signs are always placed with a purpose. Get used to reading
what they actually say. For instance if you are on a main road and
the cross-roads ahead continue in your favour then the warning sign
will say so by making the lines across narrower than the main one. If
the sign does not show this priority then you must assume that you
do not have priority to cross. Slow down and be prepared to give
way.

Warning signs are always warnings of potential danger.

Not all road signs are poles with triangles on them. If you are driving in the country in the vicinity of a stables you may well see signs of potential activity ahead of you. Fresh horse droppings must never be ignored. Two lots alongside each other definitely spell trouble – and a pair of horses riding abreast. As a new driver you may be feeling nervous, but you will certainly not be half as nervous as the novice rider on a strange horse on a country road with cars flashing past at high speed. Peter Campbell, Road Safety Officer to the British Horse Society, once told me the sad tale of the horse which jumped a hedge and landed on a large Volvo estate car. The horse was most surprised and a little upset as it galloped off into the sunset. The owner of the Volvo was faced with a very squashed and written-off motor-car. Never underestimate the weight of a horse. Like meeting trains at level crossings, always give way to, and keep well away from, something stronger than you. People who have signs in the back of their cars saying 'I slow down for Horses' may not just be horse lovers – they might be knowing car lovers too.

Road safety
Reading the road is the greatest single thing you can do to keep yourself safe when you are driving.

- Watch the way the road appears to bend in the distance.
- Look out for changes of road surface.
- Beware of the road getting narrower as you come into bends.
- Look out and allow for pedestrians on the road.
- Be aware of horses and other animals.
- On long straight stretches beware of dead ground.

Dead ground is where the road apparently goes straight on with a slight gap in the middle distance. Traffic can easily be hidden in this gap, so make sure there is no dead ground ahead of you when you are overtaking.

As you are driving along imagine the road ahead follows the shape of an ice cream cornet. Your car is based at the bottom of the cone. Behind you is a gap determined by the vehicle behind; but you hope it will always be at least two seconds' travelling time. Ahead of you lies the rest of the cornet. This is the five seconds' planning time that you always need. Remember that the first three or four seconds of space ahead of you are needed just to stop in a hurry. Five seconds will give you some time to react as well. Ten seconds gives you time to think and decide first. The ice cream in the cone is your own choice. You can have as much of it as you wish. Think in terms of at least an extra ten seconds' worth of ice cream for your safety cushion, which is what it really is. This bit allows you to look and plan much further ahead. If you really want to have the touch of luxury about your driving, remember to add the long piece of chocolate flake. This is the extension which gives you total security. Its equivalent in driving terms is the ability to look beyond the end of the road that you can see. It means looking through hedges, over fields, and across the terrain to see the way the road may be bending ahead.

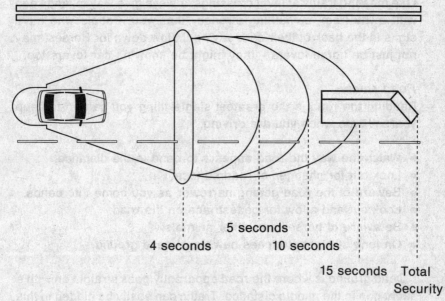

5 seconds

4 seconds   10 seconds

15 seconds   Total Security

Look – and plan – as far ahead as you can.

Remember that seeing ahead of you as far as you can is only half the story. Make sure your lights are working – even in daylight it's an offence to have broken or ineffective lights. Make sure you're easily seen and can stop safely when the need occurs. Actively plan and look ahead to see how well you can read the road. Give yourself a Brownie point when you have spotted something which others might have missed, but don't let it go to your head. Whilst you are cleverly noting one thing, there are others you may have missed. Full observation takes many years of experience, and even then most drivers, experienced or not, still miss a lot of the information which is there to be seen and used.

The road is there to be read, and if you learn how to do it properly, and keep your levels of perception high, you are well on the way to becoming an expert driver and not just a proficient one.

Coping with bends

When you are out in the country, no matter where you are you will soon come across a bend. Bends restrict your visibility and also the speed at which you drive. The rule must always be to stop safely in the distance you can see to be safe. As you drive in towards a bend you need to reduce speed so that you can always stop in that distance ahead. Try to imagine a large combine harvester trundling around the corner towards you occupying all the road. If you can't stop easily in that distance, at that speed, then you are driving too fast.

The best way to cope with bends is to take driving in three progressive stages. These are: smoothness of transmission; equal tyre grip at all times; and maximizing your position through bends.

Transmission first
Your first skill is to learn how to control the vehicle's transmission smoothly. Every time you change gear your clutch should come up slowly enough to make sure that there is no jerk at all. If each time you select a new gear the engine speed grinds or the clutch judders then you are not matching your engine speed to that of the road wheels.

Four tiny footprints of rubber tyre-tread
Once this is mastered you need to think in terms of keeping all four tyres with equal grip, all the time, on the road. This is always important, of course, because your tyre tread is the only grip that you have, but it is much more important on bends, because at this point your car wants to travel in a different direction to the way you

are turning the steering wheel. Provided the tyres grip properly all is well. However if the tread is smooth, or the road is too wet, or your speed is too fast, then your tyre grip can be lost, and the car wins.

Opening and closing bends

Straight roads are relatively rare. This is why motorways are so safe. You can see for miles at a time. On country lanes you can rarely see more than five or six hundred yards ahead of you. If your visibility projects beyond your braking distance, all is well. If the distance reduces to less than your stopping ability then you must slow down.

The final degree of driving skill concerns your ability to deal with bends. You can think of each bend as one that opens or closes as you approach. Consider the vanishing point, the point at which the parallel sides of the road appear to meet in the distance. If it appears to be moving at the same speed that you are, then the approaching bend is a neutral one, and you can maintain your speed. If you can't see any further round the corner because the vanishing point remains in the same place, then the bend is a closing one, and you must lose speed on approach. If the view round the bend is increasing as you approach then this is an opening bend, and you may be able to increase your speed through, round, and out of the bend. The amount of braking or decelerating on approach to closing bends, and the point at which you can increase your speed when coming through opening bends, are totally dependent upon the tightness or openness of the bend itself.

This is the secret of correct approach to bends at all times. It's not restricted to bends on country roads, of course, the principle applies all the time you are driving, and on all roads. Every road bends, and this vanishing point in the distance is the limit of your visibility. This the basis for all your planning, speed, and decision making.

However, where you need to discipline yourself is in the way you actually use the controls. *You must not brake on bends*. All speed changes need to be carried out whilst on the straight stretches. All you have to do on the bend is to maintain the speed you have whilst concentrating on holding the same line through the bend. Whilst you are steering you need to keep the accelerator pedal firm and steady at whatever engine speed you felt was correct. However, it is essential that you make the decision about the exact and precise speed before you start to steer through the bend. You must not change your mind halfway through a bend. If you want to go slower halfway through, it's because you selected the wrong speed to start with. Even so the safest way to is hold your speed constant, keeping the accelerator steady. Avoid sudden deceleration, even if you do want to go slower. The car is much more stable under slight acceleration than when you decelerate or brake. Hold your speed and you will hold the road. It is safer to drive through under power than to use the brakes and risk locking up or losing your line.

Next time approach a similar road just a little bit slower until you can recognize exactly what speed is safe for that type of bend, on that type of road surface and camber, in that type of vehicle.

The logical way to think it through is to start off driving through bends quite gently and only increase the speed at which you drive through them as you gain confidence.

The expert driver

These road-reading and vehicle-control skills will eventually lead you on to the final stage of driving behavioural skills, one that you will reach when you have become an expert driver, instead of just a competent or proficient one. At this stage of your driving you become aware of how you can actually adjust your steering, even though only very lightly, by increasing or decreasing the pressure on the accelerator pedal. But that is for another book.

Points to remember

- **Read the road**
- Look for early indications of what is ahead.
- Read the road as far ahead as you can.
- What sort of camber do you have and is it changing?
- Predict how the road and traffic conditions may change.
- Look for white lines, road signs, road markings, and other warnings.
- Look for pedestrians, horses, farm vehicles, mud, and other animals.

- **Treat bends with care**
- What direction do they take? Your position may need to change.
- How sharp are they? Your speed may need to be reduced.
- Bends may be sharper than you think.
- Decide if each bend is an opening, closing, or neutral one.
- Make sure your tyres maintain equal grip through each bend.

- **Mirrors and signals**
- Remember your M-S-M and P-S-L routines at all times.
- Your mirrors are your second line of observation.
- Know who is behind and what they may want to do.
- Tell others what you want to do as well.
- Sound the horn if you are sure it will help – but don't frighten the horses.

- **Overtaking**
- Only overtake when you know it is perfectly safe.
- Overtaking takes quite a long time – measure it sometime.
- Judge the speed of others correctly before committing yourself.

- **Stopping with care and thought**
- Stop when you must, but bear in mind other traffic.
- Don't stop in passing places.
- If you must park, try to pull off the road.
- Look, and signal if necessary, before you slow down.
- Wait for horses and riders; they won't be in your way for long.
- Relax and enjoy the countryside but concentrate on what matters.

4 Dual-Carriageway Driving

Dual carriageways present a complete variety of driving styles. The main thing to remember is that they do allow much greater progress, especially if they have two or more lanes in each direction, and they also mean you can (usually) ignore the thought of oncoming traffic. The real safety factor of a dual carriageway varies according to the strength of the central barrier between the carriageways. If it is a solid piece of metal and grass then it gives an added degree of security. If it's only a very simple central gap of paint, a grassy verge, or low kerbs it gives you more concern. Some dual carriageways are almost up to motorway standards, and they are often numbered A something followed by an (M) to tell the users that they are A roads but have most of a motorway's characteristics; others are simply extensions of rural single carriageways and may only last for a few hundred metres before reverting to single-carriageway status, with one lane in each direction.

Dual carriageways all have the same format. They have two or more lanes in each direction, separated by some form of barrier. They only present danger when drivers and other users forget the presence of other traffic. Motorways restrict the types of vehicles and road users who can use them, and most of these can move at the same speed; dual carriageways can have pedestrians, horses, milk floats, cycles, and all manner of road users, each of them moving at their own individual pace.

Speed is your first impression. Much more concentration is needed to assess, and continually reassess, the speed and position of all other traffic around you. If the speed of the traffic is constant the actual speed you're travelling doesn't matter so much. It is change of speed and variations of speed between different types of traffic which create danger.

Joining and leaving

In many cases you simply continue driving along a road and it becomes a dual carriageway after a signed warning. When you see the sign you will know that the dual carriageway starts within the distance which may be shown on the sign, or that you are almost on it already.

Joining from the left

Entering dual carriageways with a left turn is easy. It means you only have to concentrate on what is happening on your right. Once you can see the easy opportunity to enter you can join the road and catch up with the speed of the traffic already on it. You don't need to worry quite so much about any traffic on your left which may be overtaking on the wrong side of the road.

Occasionally you can also enter a dual carriageway with the intention of turning right. Now you have to make a decision quite early on, whether you can wait in the gap between the two lanes of traffic. The answer to this is simple. If you can get into the centre reservation safely, and there is room to wait without interfering with traffic coming from either direction, then you should do so. If waiting means your tail or nose is stuck in the path of oncoming traffic, then you should not do so. Remember, too, that you have to give way to traffic on your left intending to turn right in front of you to enter the road you are leaving. They may not be willing to give room for you, and their priority is greater than yours. If it is you turning right from the dual carriageway you need to look for anyone who is blocking your path coming from your right. Even if you have priority, you can't always rely on it, and must never insist on it.

If you are joining from a side road on the left you may even find you have a slip road just like a motorway; the rules for joining by slip roads are explained on p. 61.

> ### *Joining from the right*
> **Unlike motorways, it is possible to join dual carriageways from the right as well as left. The greatest danger is crossing the path of fast-moving traffic in the right-hand lanes in both directions. If you are entering from a side road which crosses the dual carriageway you are allowed to wait in the gap, provided you can do so without exposing your front or rear to traffic on your right or left. If there is not enough room you should not go. On occasions it will be necessary to pull halfway across without this guarantee, but this is best avoided if at all possible.**
>
> **When you do join the road, make sure you can get into the left lane and keep the right-hand lanes clear for fast-moving traffic, which will insist on overtaking. If you are driving on a dual carriageway and see traffic joining from your right ahead, take extra care that you do not get caught out in a position of overtaking them in the left lane as they chug gently along in the outside lane.**

Reading the road

Reading the road ahead is just as important on these roads as it is on single carriageways, and except for oncoming traffic and the possibilities for overtaking, the same rules apply. Effective and constant observation is essential. Early and planned use of all the mirrors will enable you to be aware of who is closing up on you, who wants to overtake, and who is content to hang on your tail. By using your mirrors well you can also tell who is hiding in your blind spots. Good drivers are able to know who is around them, even if they are temporarily out of sight, because they were watching them close up ready to overtake.

Forward observation is important too. Because the overall speed of some sections of the traffic is likely to be higher and some will still be limited, the need and opportunities to overtake are much greater.

Much more effort is needed to ensure that you are aware of all other traffic – especially those who concern you most.

What you need is the ability to keep your concentration at its highest point without becoming so stressed that the driving is hard work. You can only do this if you drive to a system. Earlier, on p. 32, we looked at this one:

Full Observation and Information in and out
Position then **Speed** then **Gears**

It's just as important on dual carriageways.

Give yourself space
Space, visibility, and time all form part of your driving pattern. If you maintain this pattern you will always be safe and keep others as safe as possible too. The first rule of space in driving is to know that you are totally responsible for the distance between you and the vehicle ahead at all times. Never drive closer than you know you can stop.

It's not always possible to have the same control over the traffic alongside you, as you are more dependent upon the width of the lanes, and the nature of the traffic. But you do have the power to drop back if it is not possible to drive past them. Choose who you are happy to be alongside, and if you don't like the situation, change it.

It's also less easy to control the traffic behind you. However, if you find you are being bullied by vehicles behind, or if they are getting too close, you can compensate for it by decelerating and increasing the gap ahead of you. The car behind is more likely to run into the back of you if you are closing up your own following distance. If in doubt extend this gap. Create that safety cushion around you until it is as safe as your speed allows.

Remember, your speed must decrease to match a shrinking safety cushion. Your speed can only increase if the safety cushion expands to match.

Increase your visibility
The first rule of visibility is to make sure you can see far enough ahead of you. It is not enough to be able to see what the vehicle

ahead is doing, even if you have a safe braking distance between you. You need to look beyond the traffic ahead so that you can plan for what they may be doing soon too.

At 30 m.p.h. in a busy traffic situation you must have your driving path laid out in front of you for several hundred feet. Just as when you walk upstairs you look ahead and not at where your feet are going, so in the car you need to look ten or more seconds into the distance in order to plan. Don't look where you are now, but where you will be when your planning reaches culmination. You also need to get the whole picture of what is happening, ten or more seconds ahead of you. It is not enough to focus down the path which your wheels will be following. Look and take in what is happening in the whole of that cone of visibility ahead of you. Only then can you filter out what is less likely to matter, and concentrate on the things that will affect you. Consider everything that is ahead of you and discard what is not needed. Make your plans for what you will need to do in five, ten, and fifteen seconds' time.

In order to do this you must always keep your eyes moving, trying not to focus on any one thing. This is particularly dangerous on dual carriageways. Many drivers seem to fix their gaze on the vehicle ahead, and find themselves mesmerized by it to such an extent that when it stops they use the brakes of the vehicle ahead to stop. The drivers argue they were unlucky; but all nose to tail shunts are avoidable by holding back before the panic ensues.

Tailgating (driving too close) and staring into space at someone's rear lights as you follow the vehicle ahead are the basic causes of the most common of these accidents. Drivers see the brake lights come on, but don't register in time to stop safely. As a result twenty or more vehicles can all plough into the back of each other simply because of the additional action of the leading vehicle. The cause is not the initial sudden braking, but close following. By holding back and looking further ahead there would not have been any need for subsequent urgent and panic braking.

Use your peripheral distant vision in order to take in the maximum amount of information. Move your head as well as your eyes. You must filter out what is not needed, but you can only filter it out when you have seen it. This is known as selectively seeing. Your visual perception needs to be trained. It is not enough to open your eyes and stare into the middle distance somewhere up ahead.

You need to train yourself to *look* where you are going; to *see* what concerns you and your intentions; to *observe* everything that can change or aid your current plans; and to *perceive* what could be out of sight, but likely to happen soon.

Once you have seen something which will affect you, your driving plan, your system of position, speed, and gears, must come into play. If you perceive a hazard ahead there are only three things which you can do to cope with it.

- Adjust your speed, usually by slowing down to give you time;
- Change your direction in order to pass or miss the hazard;
- Give a signal, by lights, horn, indicators, by position or by arm.

You must avoid getting into a potentially dangerous situation by one of these ways.

Slowing down includes stopping.
Changing direction includes reversing if necessary.
Signalling includes using your position to indicate your presence.

Points to remember

- Take extra care when you join high-speed traffic.
- Although dual carriageways do not have two-way traffic – still look out.
- Practise your visual search and decision-making skills.
- Take extra care on roundabouts not to join an exit instead of an entrance.
- Watch out for traffic emerging on your right and then hold back.
- When overtaking expect traffic; but don't expect them to drop back for you.
- Remember to drop your speed when you revert to single carriageways.
- Your mirrors are even more important at speed.
- Speed limits on dual carriageways do vary. If a lower speed is signed there must be a good reason for it.

BREAKDOWNS ON BUSY ROADS

If your car stops whilst you are driving the three likely causes are fuel, electrics, or mechanical.

1 Pull in to the left. Even try to coast out of gear to get away from the main stream of traffic. Get off the road if you can and switch on your hazard lights (if they don't work it's certainly your electrics at fault). Use a warning triangle if you have one and it might safeguard the scene (50 metres behind you).

2 Try to find out what is wrong. If it's obvious and you can do something about it, get it done quickly and safely. If you can't do anything about it, call the breakdown services, your own favourite garage man, or find the nearest dealer or garage to where you are.

   If you have a car phone now is the time to use it. Say exactly where you are, and where you will be when the breakdown truck arrives. (They won't do anything to your car if you're not there.) No phone? Walk to the nearest call box, or in desperation knock on a door of the nearest house. Wear warm clothes, flat shoes, and a light or reflective armband at night. If you have children, take them with you; but leave pets in the car with adequate ventilation.

   Lock the doors and keep the keys with you. Get a garage to help, and tell friends or family where you are. If necessary ask the police to help. If you are a lone female, the motoring services and police will give you priority.

3 Once you have asked for help decline any offers from passing motorists and use very careful judgement about offers of any kind. If in doubt you are better off waiting for a breakdown truck than almost anything else.

   When the breakdown truck arrives confirm the identity of the organization and the driver or mechanic.

AVOID
- Letting other people play with your car; they might damage it.
- Driving when you know you have a potential fault on your car.
- Driving on lonely roads with a dodgy motor.
- Driving without a spare wheel and wheel-changing kit.
- Leaving a broken down car for a long time.
- Opening the window more than you need to speak to people.
- Standing in the road waving traffic down.
- Panicking: think rationally and keep your cool.

ALWAYS
- Keep some loose change for the phone in the car. Better still, carry a portable phone. They are cheap enough to have one for breakdowns or emergencies.
- Join a motoring organization. The cost of breaking down and getting a tow back home can be quite expensive.
- Keep to main roads and well-lit roads at night.
- Carry a torch, maps, and means of keeping warm in winter.
- Pull in at a garage or service station if you think your car sounds odd.
- Be wary of helpful strangers.
- Look for the safest place to wait. If you stay in the car lock the doors.
- Ask the mechanic for *your* name when he arrives.
- Plan what you would do in a breakdown before it happens.

5 Motorway Driving

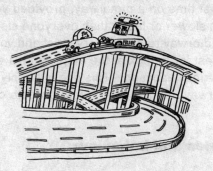

Many new drivers worry about their first time alone on a motorway. Even those who have taken a few professional lessons after their test still realize that there's a difference between going on a motorway for the first time and driving on them for the first time – alone. Motorways are safer, but they are also faster than normal roads, and because of this although there are long boring stretches, sometimes things do happen quicker, and there is a need for great concentration on the potential for change.

There are also two types of motorways. The Department of Transport calls them rural and urban motorways. You need to think of them as quiet and busy. Quiet motorways can be boring, and your greatest need is for attention to the road and traffic conditions way ahead. Busy motorways can have so many things happening on them that your attention is needed all around you rather than just focused ahead.

Motorways are like dual carriageways, only safer. They are safer for three reasons. The first one is that traffic is restricted to those who can make best use of it. Pedestrians, cyclists, small motorbikes and mopeds, most slow-moving vehicles, L drivers (except for LGV), agricultural vehicles, and animals, are all banned. They are also safer because they are straighter. You can see much further ahead, lanes are wider, there are always two or more lanes in each direction, and plenty of warning signs; but no sharp bends, oncoming traffic, traffic turning right or roundabouts.

However the most important reason why motorways are so safe is that generally speaking every road user on them is travelling in the same direction, and at a similar speed: every vehicle in each lane of traffic is normally moving at the same sort of speed as every other in that lane.

So for your first time on a motorway, provided you don't want to drive very much slower or faster than everyone else, you will enjoy your trip. The motorway rules are very strict and you're not allowed to stop – for a rest, or to look at the map – so it's essential to plan your motorway trips in advance. This doesn't apply just to your first time on a motorway, but every time you go onto one.

Motorway rules and behaviour

There are a number of basic rules which you must always obey if you are to be safe, and to keep others safe, whilst you are driving on Britain's safest roads. These rules apply to the way you join and enter, drive along and maintain lane discipline, overtake, change motorways, leave, and adjust to normal roads again.

Motorways all have the same format and are built to very high standards. They are not allowed to be used by certain classes of road users – mainly those who would not benefit from being on them – and they have many additional safety features which make them the safest roads to drive on. Motorways are always dual carriageways, and have large solid central reservations to separate the two directions of traffic. They also have hard shoulders on the left of the two, three or more lanes which go in each direction. These must be left free for police and other emergency service vehicles.

The lanes are always wide, and well marked, and as they are usually straight for long distances, you can see much further ahead of you. Even on busy motorways the general speed of traffic is much higher than on roads where there are pedestrians, cyclists and milk floats all vying for space. On urban motorways each lane of traffic has an electronic signal system which only applies to traffic in that lane. The message can be changed to suit the traffic conditions and is shown on overhead gantries. Great care needs to be taken to make sure you know what the various signals mean and how to obey them.

Motorway information signs are also used with increasing frequency. Some signals, especially in the M25 area, actually warn you of specific problems, like hold ups, or accidents ahead, so that even if you can't get off the motorway at least you know why there is a queue of traffic. Many of these signals can be used to control the speed of the traffic flow.

Vehicles are not allowed to reverse, to cross the central reservation, or to drive in the wrong direction on motorways. Because the exits and entrances are limited, if you find you are travelling in the wrong direction, you must continue to the next exit and get off there. The general speed of motorway driving necessitates extra care with following distances, braking, observation, signalling and overtaking.

Joining the motorway

A number of motorways actually start at the end of an A road. In these cases you are driving along and carry on doing so as you pass a sign telling non-motorway traffic they must leave at the oncoming exit. Those wishing to continue along the motorways just stay in the lane they are already in. Your only awareness of the motorway is that the roads suddenly seem to be wider and easier to drive on.

You usually join a motorway from roundabouts and main A roads by means of a slip road. This leads to an acceleration lane, and from this you need to enter lane one (the left lane) fitting in with other traffic already on the motorway. The obvious rule here is not to interfere in any way with traffic already on the motorway. Make sure that your speed fits in with theirs as soon as possible. Vehicles already on a motorway usually realize it makes sense to move into lane two as they approach an entrance, in order to make room for traffic trying to join.

You must avoid entering the slip road and acceleration lanes so quickly that you're forced to brake and stop before you can join. Apart from following traffic hitting you in the rear, you will also find it more difficult to pick up speed quickly. Try to enter at the same speed as the traffic ahead and behind you in lane one. Then you can merge in with them and adjust your speed and position to suit your own braking distance. Mirrors and signals must be used correctly to avoid interfering with following traffic, and full and proper observation as you enter usually involves looking over your right shoulder as well as using door mirrors – don't rely on mirrors alone. Apart from anything else you may be grateful for as much eye contact as possible with oncoming drivers and riders. You should always allow motorcyclists the same distances, space, and courtesies you would to any car or truck driver.

Lane discipline

When driving along motorways always remain in lane one unless you are travelling faster than traffic ahead of you and it is safe to move into either of the overtaking lanes (lanes two and three). If you do use these lanes you must return to lane one as soon as it is safe and convenient.

Regrettably, many more experienced motorists, those who should know better, try to stay in the overtaking lanes for normal driving. This is bad practice, and causes inconvenience and tailbacks, and annoys other users. These drivers are sometimes known as 'Founder-members of the Middle Lane Owners' Club'. They are easily identified by the way they ignore other traffic, avoid the empty lanes on their left, never use their mirrors, and only signal after they have done something. They also tend to drive in bunches and tailgate each other like lemmings looking for their happy ending. Treat them as accident material, and keep well clear of them: the safest way is to stay in the left lane at a safe and suitable speed until you are able to get past them safely should you need to.

Two problems are caused by these drivers, and made worse by the traffic congestion which is part of the current motorway system. All drivers seem to drive too closely to each other. They have never heard of the two-second rule, and they like to read the shirt-collar label of the driver in front. The two-second rule is sometimes made a physical reality on a number of motorways by the painting of white chevrons on the road surface. When these appear you must aim to have at least two chevrons in view between you and the vehicle ahead at any time and this will give you ample room to brake gently should the need arise. But even two seconds from the vehicle is too close under most motorway driving conditions. Four seconds will give you time to relax and to react easily. You will also have to take into account the ability of the truck or other large vehicle following too closely behind you to stop, and you need to double your four-second gap if the traffic is fast and furious.

You will notice that they never paint these chevrons in the outside lane (lane three) of motorways. It could be that the outside lane is never clear enough of traffic to carry out the painting. Or perhaps it is thought that those who stick in this lane all the time are past redemption? Two seconds is never enough. Imagine the vehicle in front stopping dead. Will you stop? Or stop dead?

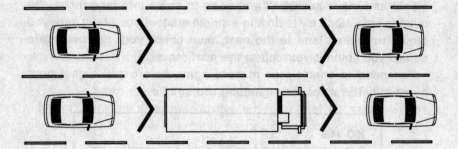

Always keep at least two chevrons (or a similar distance) between you and the vehicle you are following.

Overtaking

The two-second rule only ever applies if everything else is perfect, and that has to include the reactions of the driver behind you too. On motorways bear in mind that safest of all rules when driving: *Never be fourth in a queue of traffic*.

If you find you're driving along in any stream of traffic and you can count more than two cars closely ahead of you, drop back. Give yourself that additional edge. If the leading car has to stop it could be for any reason at all. The second driver needs to have full concentration in order to stop quickly and still safely. The third vehicle will have to perform an emergency stop in order to stop in time. The fourth car will either crunch into the third, or if very skilful and lucky, will stop about a metre or so from it. If there is a fifth vehicle following closely behind that, it will push the fourth car into the third one anyway! Never be fourth in a queue. Be the leader of the next queue, five or ten seconds behind the others.

In theory you can stay in the left-hand lane all the time you are on the motorway until you need to get into the deceleration lane to leave. In practice you are bound to find some slower-moving vehicles and will need to change lanes. Remember that that traffic coming up behind you could be driving well in excess of the speed limit, so a single look in your mirrors is not enough. You will need to make constant reference to them before you can safely decide to signal and move across. If you need to move into lane three, the outside lane, don't try to do it in a single manoeuvre. Make sure you move from each lane to the next, then check your mirrors again before you commit yourself to the next move.

You need to check your mirrors again before you signal your move out. The rules for signalling are simple.

HC 168
Remember that traffic may be coming up behind you very quickly. Signal before you move out.

It doesn't mention signalling to move back in, though. Think about signals for a moment. You need to signal if anyone can benefit from seeing it. In the case of moving out, the vehicle you are overtaking, as well as any others, will obviously benefit from being told so. A signal is a must. Then cancel it. Keep an eye on your mirrors as you get past the vehicles you have started to overtake. Make sure you see them, first in your left door mirror, then in your main mirror. Even then, take your time before you get back in. At 70 m.p.h. you need about a hundred metres to stop comfortably. If you pull back into the left in less than that distance you will upset the braking distance of the driver you have just overtaken. Give plenty of room for them to continue without forcing them to brake.

There is no need to signal you are getting back into the lane on the left, unless it is really necessary. The only occasions you may need to do so are if you become aware of a fast moving car coming up behind you and you want to reassure the driver that you are getting out of its way quickly. You may also need an urgent left indicator signal if your car has a problem and you desperately need to get onto the hard shoulder for safety reasons. Save your left signals for really urgent occasions. After all the rule of the road is *Keep Left*. If you intend to get back in then no one will be surprised provided you do so sensibly and not too close to the vehicle you have just overtaken. A left indicator used after an overtaking manoeuvre might be seen as a sign that you are now going to brake and turn left at the next exit, or to pull in to the hard shoulder. Both of these impressions might make someone worry and brake suddenly causing confusion and mayhem to the traffic behind.

Even after you have overtaken a whole stream of traffic you still need not signal your intention to return to the left. Returning to the left lane should be an automatic follow up to using the overtaking lanes for their proper purpose.

A reasonable guide to whether you have time to move back in to the left each time you overtake when the vehicles are all some distance apart, is to count to yourself how long you are likely to remain in the left lane before moving out again. If it means getting back into the left for MORE than 15 seconds, then get back in. If you expect to move out again in less than 15 seconds, and there is no other traffic behind you which will be inconvenienced, then stay out and continue in the overtaking lane.

So if you actually overtake a slower moving vehicle every 15 seconds or less and are not being pushed by faster moving traffic yourself, you can stay in the middle or outside lane.

Signs and signals

Whilst you are driving along remember that there are all kinds of signals. You need to look ahead at all times for warning signs. There will be those given on the official warning boards. On rural motorways they are usually shown in the central reservation every two miles or so. On urban motorways signals are displayed on gantries overhead, with the potential to signal separately for users of every lane.

There are other signals and signs too. Other road users will be giving signals all the time. Some of them will be genuine Highway Code signals. They may even use them correctly, but you cannot guarantee this. The secret is to read into other people's indicators not so much what the Highway Code says but what the drivers actually mean. For example, quite often a right indicator does't mean, 'I am waiting until it is clear to pull out into the next lane,' it means, 'Look out, here I come.' In some very bad cases it even means 'LOOK OUT, I'VE ALREADY COME OUT!'

Distractions cause disasters

Look out for drivers ahead or alongside who are not paying attention to what they should be doing. Quite often you will discover heated discussions, snogging passengers (with the driver), fighting children, distraught mothers, furious fathers, map-reading solitary motorists, and dozing drivers, all of whom are competing for space and places on the roads with you. If you do suspect lack of concentration or attention to the driving task by drivers around you, don't compound the risk. Drop back and keep out of their way. Only overtake them when you are really sure it is safe.

Look out too for the driver who overtakes, then signals left and pulls in directly in front of you. It may be carelessness or just stupidity; but it might also mean the driver wants to exit to the left very soon. That driver's next action will most likely be to brake; and he has already decimated your previously safe braking distance.

Watch out for direction signs. When planning your motorway trip make sure you know exactly what exit you want, and then practise the countdown to it, so that you are not taken by surprise. If the journey is a long one, make sure you know where the service stations are, and plan to stop at one or more of them at no more than two-hour intervals. Motorway service stations are not renowned for their cheap petrol prices, nor is their food likely to reach the highest standards, but the loos are very convenient indeed. Even if you and your passengers don't need a comfort stop it is good to stretch your legs, relax your eyes and physically switch off for ten minutes or so.

The hard shoulder

Stopping on the hard shoulder is forbidden at any time. You should never pull in for any reason except emergencies and breakdowns. The definition of a genuine emergency can cover a whole list of things. My view of what constitutes an emergency is a matter which, if not resolved quickly, will cause the driver to lose control or concentration. So, a child feeling sick (or being sick) in the back seat is not a real emergency provided you have another adult in the car capable of directing the flow. If you are the only adult, and they are seriously distracting you from your driving, then you could pull in briefly in order to sort things out. Being sick is not an excuse to remain on the hard shoulder for more than a few minutes at the most.

Feeling tired is not an excuse either. If you are feeling tired and are really unable to make it to the next exit then you could pull onto the hard shoulder, get out of the car (SAFELY), open the bonnet perhaps, get some fresh air, walk away from the car by stepping over the safety barrier and take a few long, hard, cold breaths of air.

None of this should last for more than three minutes at the most. Close the bonnet, get back into the driving seat and then drive on to the next exit. This procedure is safer than driving whilst tired – and dozing off even momentarily. But it is not an excuse to pull onto the hard shoulder and take a nap. Survivors are not treated kindly by the police and magistrates. Incidentally, the purpose of the open bonnet whilst you are getting some air does two things. It draws attention to the fact that you are stopped; and it might just enable you to convince any passing patrol car driver that it is your engine which is the weak link in your personal safety chain at that time. The hard shoulder should not be used for waiting, driving, or overtaking. It must be kept clear for police and other services to use in the event of an emergency. If you are stuck in a blockage and there is no likelihood of early movement you must not use the hard shoulder to escape even if others around you are doing so. The only time you can use it is if you are told to do so by signs or by the motorway police. Should you have a problem with your car, or if one of the children is being sick, then you are allowed to pull in temporarily to resolve the situation. But beware of trying to work under the bonnet, walking all round the car, or stepping into the fast-moving stream in the left lane. If you can't get your car started within two or three minutes get help.

Breakdowns on motorways

If you have kept your vehicle well maintained and fuelled up, and carried out a thorough additional check before you left, you should be in no danger of breaking down on a motorway. However things can always go wrong and you need to know what to do if you do have to pull into the hard shoulder and await a breakdown repair or towaway truck.

Get out of the car

If you have to wait, don't wait in the car. If you have passengers and children with you get them out of the car, off the hard shoulder, over the barrier and as far away from danger as possible. Do this before you go for the telephone. Never stay in the car or leave anyone else in it either. You may have read horror stories about being attacked whilst broken-down. You may have heard about the dangers of letting other motorists apparently offer to help you before they turn nasty. The real statistics are even nastier than you might think. But they are nothing to do with being attacked.

The chances of being attacked on a motorway are less than one in five hundred million. The chances of a broken down vehicle which is on the hard shoulder for more than twenty minutes being run into from behind by a dozing driver are something like one in twenty thousand. This is why you do not wait in your vehicle; and you must never, ever try to work on the right-hand side of the car with your backside sticking out into the left lane. Dozing drivers fix their eyes on the road ahead. If a truck driver has been at the wheel a long time he could easily mistake you for a car moving in the left lane and follow you.

If your vehicle breaks down in the outside lanes, and you are unable to get onto the hard shoulder it is even more important to get away from your car. But only do this when you are sure it is safe to do so. Remain in the car, do not put any warning triangle out, but do stay belted up until you know you can get out and across the carriageway to safety. If you have broken down alongside the central reservation it may make sense to stand between the two layers of Armco fencing. (This is the very heavy metal shielding used to keep traffic from crossing the reservation.) But this is only an option if you cannot cross the lanes to the hard shoulder and safety on the embankment away from the traffic altogether. You may have to wait for the police to arrive to rescue you from your little Armco prison.

If you are disabled or unable to move out of the car for any reason, switch on your hazard lights, and try to display a help sign. You can get signs that can be displayed in the rear windows of vehicles asking for help. There is a very good help sign in the form of a sunshade which serves as an accident warning when needed and to keep the sun off the inside of a parked car in normal use.

The emergency phones
There is always an emergency phone within half a mile of any spot on the motorway. Next, look at the arrows on the nearest post and remember as closely as you can where you are to identify the spot to the emergency services when you are put through to them. Walk briskly to the phone, staying as close to the barrier on the hard shoulder as possible. The phones are free to use, and connect you straight to the police force which controls that stretch of motorway. Face the oncoming traffic, give them your name and car number, also any details of membership of breakdown associations you may have. They will then tell you to return to your vehicle and wait with it for the breakdown services to reach you. Do not get back into the car, but stay on the embankment, or as far from the traffic as you can, but where you can see and be seen. If you are a woman alone, say so at the start and you do get additional priority. If you have a personal phone with you it is perhaps better to use this initially. However the police prefer you to use their roadside phones to confirm your exact position.

Changing motorways

When you see your exit coming up it may not necessarily be a normal motorway exit: in many cases these days you can switch from one motorway to another without actually getting off the motorway system. The rules are the same. Know beforehand at which number exit your motorway change occurs. Watch the road and route signs and get into lane early. On most occasions you will find that you need to get into the left-hand lanes of your present motorway to travel to the right, and into the right-hand lanes if your new motorway takes you off to the left. This will confuse you on your first outings, but when you see the natural geography of motorway junctions you will realize why there are so many mini-Spaghetti Junctions at motorway intersections.

Leaving a motorway

If you're just getting off the motorway in order to revert to ordinary roads the normal procedure is to look for the first advance warning about one mile from it. This often gives an exit number and the road numbers which connect to the motorway at that point. At half a mile from the exit a second sign identifies the towns which are fed by those roads. Then at 300 yards from the deceleration lane there is the three line countdown marker; followed by the two line one at 200 yards and a single line marker 100 yards from the deceleration lane. It is at the 100 yard marker that you should normally begin to use your left indicator signal to say you are turning off.

Only when you have crossed into the deceleration lane should you begin to slow down and fit in with the traffic around you. The deceleration lane leads into a slip road which is normally two lanes wide. You will probably need the left lane unless you are intending to go right at the end, in which case choose the right lane here. Get into the correct lane early, and make sure your speed suits the traffic conditions at the end of the slip road. You may have to cope with traffic lights, or a roundabout, or you may even find yourself emerging onto a busy trunk road. In any case it is essential that you take extra care with your speed.

It is so easy to drive at high speeds when you are on motorways that you may find you haven't adjusted yourself to the lower speeds of ordinary roads soon enough. After driving at 60 or 70 m.p.h. for a long time 30 m.p.h. seems almost crawling.

HC 186
Your speed may be higher than you think – 50 mph may feel like 30 mph. Check your speedometer and adjust your speed accordingly.

Once you get back on to ordinary roads again, even if they are dual carriage-ways, you need to watch your speed until you are acclimatized to the new lower speeds on this road. Don't forget too, that these roads are likely to have roundabouts, oncoming traffic from various directions, and sharp bends on them.

Points to remember

- Know where you are going, and which exit you want.
- Remember which motorway numbers you need.

- Extend your observation much further forward.
- Keep safe following distances.
- Use motorway signs to aid your planning.
- Keep in the left lane as much as you can.
- Avoid driving for too long; take a break.
- What to do if your car breaks down.
- Know how to get off the motorway earlier in jams or holdups.
- Let someone know where you are going; and tell them when you expect to arrive.

MOTORWAY RULES

Always plan your journey.
Check your vehicle – and yourself – before you start.
Watch your speed.
Keep your distance.

There is no such thing as a fast lane – or a slow lane – on a motorway.
Keep to the left lane (lane one) unless you need to pull out or overtake.
If you overtake, allow plenty of room and time before you get back in.
Use your mirrors like crazy.
Keep your eyes moving all the time.
Know where everyone else is, especially when they disappear into your blindspots.

Remember the stopping distances and double them when on motorways.
Speed limits are limits not targets; but try to maintain the same speed as others in your lane.
Silly overtakers often need speedy undertakers.

Roadworks on motorways are a pain; but not as much as those who insist on overtaking in the face of closing lanes and cones.
But if you are overtaken, let the overtakers in.

Know and understand what the motorway matrix signs mean.
In bad weather double your normal safety distances, and in very bad weather stay home if you can.
Always listen to radio broadcasts on traffic and weather information.

Long-distance driving can be boring. Occupy your brain by concentrating on safe driving. If it is a help you can pace yourself by changing your speed, or style of driving, every ten minutes or so.

Never drive for more than an hour or two without a break. Plan your breaks to suit your journey. If you can change drivers to give yourself a rest this helps too.

If you are taking children in the car with you, make sure they have plenty to occupy themselves with, and don't allow yourself to be distracted by them.

6 Night Driving

Driving at night is sometimes a cause for concern for some drivers. You may have had only a few lessons in the dark, if any, with a professional driving instructor. Quite often the only experience you have had of night driving will have been in town, with excellent street lighting, when there was hardly any difference between driving in daylight and at night. Suddenly you will have to drive for the first time in the dark, and along country lanes with no street lighting at all. What should you do?

Fortunately, once you have done it, successfully, you will realize that not only is it not a real problem, but it some ways it can be more relaxing than driving in daytime. There are fewer distractions, and your concentration can be much more relaxed, provided you always bear in mind the need for safe stopping distances.

Night-time visibility

The rules for night driving are the same as for driving in daylight.

> **HC 57**
> **Drive at a speed that will allow you to stop well within the distance you can see to be clear.**

This rule applies just as much at night as it does during the day. Remember if you cannot see, you must slow down or stop.

This means that you must drive within the limits of any street lighting, and your own headlights, at all times. If you have problems seeing at night have your night vision tested. Some people, especially as they get older, find that their daytime vision is still all right, but their night vision is very bad. Get it checked anyway. It might save a life. If you wear glasses make sure they're always clean.

Driving at night at 60 m.p.h. means that you must be able to see that the road ahead is safe for a distance of more than 240 feet (nearly 75 metres). You must be able to see at least eighteen car lengths of clear road ahead of you. Yet if you're driving on country roads in the dark where the 60 m.p.h. national speed limit is in force the odds are there are no lights except for those on your car. Can you safely stop in the distance you can clearly see to be safe? If not, then your maximum speed limit is not 60 m.p.h., but is restricted to your safe braking distance.

You can't rely on other vehicles and road users being well lit. Youngsters often dress up in dark clothing because it doesn't show the dirt, and because it's fashionable – it probably isn't cool to wear a reflective armband when you're on your way to a date or to the pub. Many cyclists are quite content to ride without lights whilst wearing dark clothing. Some pub customers stagger home from their nights out, quite happy knowing that there is no blood-alcohol limit for pedestrians. Unfortunately they then rely on the extra wits, driving skills, and keen observation of drivers around them.

Don't be blind

Many people who drive at night do so quite blindly. They take it for granted that no one would be hiding in a hedge or behind a tree, and that every cyclist and pedestrian is wearing bright clothing and carries brilliant lights. This is far from the truth, and you can never accept that other road users will make life easy for you. You need to look on every road user as a fool waiting to involve you in their own stupidity, carelessness, and eventual accidents.

Of course you will know that your headlights are all working and correctly focused. You know they show you as much of the road ahead as possible. But even so there are a great many blind spots ahead of you. Trees and bushes cause bad shadows. Parked vehicles hide other road users. Are your lights clean? Is your vehicle weighed down at the back? Is your windscreen clean and clear? There's no point in having good lights if you can't see through the windows.

Did you know that most main beam headlamps can only show a clear view – if the road is straight – for about 250 feet? The minimum stopping distance at 60 m.p.h. is 240 feet.

So in theory, on a good night, in a good car, with good tyres and brakes, on a good road surface, a good driver might just manage to pull up in the distance the driver can see to be safe.

However if any of the factors are not good then the minimum distance needed to stop must be doubled, trebled, or even multiplied by ten or more. What do you know about the condition of the tyres, the road surface, the brakes – and yourself?

Most importantly of all, how good is a good driver, and are any of us as good as we think we are?

Does age and experience affect night driving?
Age certainly has a great effect on driving. Experience also affects our abilities to drive at night. We need the experience of having done it before, to give us confidence. But experience is wasted if you don't learn from it. Older drivers – those in their late fifties and sixties – need more light to see the same things at night as a twenty-year-old. Similarly older people's eyes take much longer to recover from glare than youngsters', and because of this their eyes have to work much harder, which makes night driving much more tiring for older drivers. But lack of experience also means you need to concentrate harder. This too is tiring, so give yourself a break.

Almost the worst possible scenario for any driving situation would be that of a new sixty year-old-driver with no night-time driving experience in a strange car and a town which has changed a lot. Even worse, dangerously so, are those experienced, young, fast drivers whose minds are elsewhere while they are driving at any time.

Younger people usually have the benefit of quicker reactions, both physically and optically. But an inexperienced driver doesn't always know where to look for danger. What is needed is concentration on the driving task. Sensible experience allows you to filter out what is not needed. You must always drive within the limits of your vision, your lights, and your abilities. The best eyesight – and the quickest reactions – in the world will not help if the driver is not looking for, and anticipating, danger.

Use your experience to help you in the future. Experience helps us to know where to look, and can lead to more relaxed driving. Gain experience and learn from it, just as you did from your driving lessons.

Use your lights to see and be seen

The time to switch your lights on is whenever you would be grateful to see lights on an oncoming car. Don't wait until you can hardly see in the encircling gloom before switching them on. Car lights cost nothing to run. But you need them on for others to see you, as much as you do to have them light up the road ahead for you.

Dipped or main beam?
Always use the best lighting you have. This means using main beam lights when you can, but using dipped headlights if you are behind another driver, or have someone coming towards you.

HC 132
You should . . . dip your headlights when meeting vehicles or other road users and before you dazzle the driver of a vehicle you are following.

When you have to use dipped lights, slow down. If your vision is suddenly reduced you need to cut your speed to keep your braking distance under control. The view afforded by dipped lights is much, much less than for main beam. Only go back to main beam if you know you will not dazzle other road users.

Some cars are fitted with additional lights: they are not needed for any normal driving purposes. Using low-slung lights is illegal except in falling snow or fog. And, of course, many of those additional rally-style driving lights fixed to the grilles of ageing Ford Escorts are only for show and serve no normal driving purpose.

Rear fog lights

All new cars are fitted with at least one high intensity rear fog-light. It is controlled by a separate switch on the dashboard, and there is also a warning light showing when these lights are on. Yet it is amazing how many cars still have these lights switched on in daylight when it is raining, or at night when there is no fog at all. The brightness of these lights is considerable. Next time it's raining or foggy, compare the difference in brightness between the normal tail-lights on a car and those of these high intensity lights designed to make vehicles more clearly seen from the rear. On a bad night you can easily see these one or two bright-red fog-lights long before the normal rear lights appear.

Then notice how dazzling these high-intensity lights can be to following drivers in good driving conditions. Not only is it dangerous to use them wrongly, it is also a motoring offence, and you can be prosecuted for having them lit when the conditions are not suitable.

If your car doesn't have rear fog-lights fitted as standard they are very cheap to buy, relatively easy to fit, and only slightly awkward to wire up. The law says that they must be fitted with a warning light visible to the driver and they can only be switched on when dipped or main headlights are also in use. Provided you can make sure that they comply with the law, and you don't leave them on at the wrong times, it is worthwhile having them fitted.

HC 133
Use fog lights when visibility is seriously reduced, generally when you cannot see for more than 100 metres (328 ft). You MUST NOT use fog lights at other times.

Hazard warning lights

All new vehicles are fitted with hazard warning lights too. These are operated by a bright red switch, sometimes on the dashboard, occasionally near the steering wheel. The hazard lights flash left and right indicators at the same time, and should only be used when you need to tell other road users of additional danger. They can be switched on when you are stationary, or temporarily obstructing other traffic. They can also be used, with great care, when you are moving. This can only be done on motorways, or dual carriageways with a 70 m.p.h. limit, when you need to inform following traffic of problems ahead. Do not keep them flashing for very long – just long enough for the traffic behind to wake up and take notice. And of course you would never use them as a cover for illegal or danger-ous parking. Would you?

High-level brake lights
Some vehicles are fitted with extra brake lights in the rear windows of their cars. These can be beneficial, not so much to drivers who are immediately behind but to vehicles four or five spaces back. Other drivers can see the brake lights come on, through the various windows ahead of them, and get advance warning of slowing down.

Flashing headlights at night
Everyone knows that you should never use your headlights as signals to other road users. This is certainly so during the day, when the signal could easily be misinterpreted, but in darkness, especially when it's illegal to sound your horn anyway, it can be helpful to flash your lights before you arrive at cross-roads or junctions, or when approaching bends, to warn any traffic out of sight of your presence on the road.

Don't dazzle, and avoid being dazzled
Dazzle is caused by many things. One of the worst causes can be your own dirty windscreen. If it is clear and clean it will reduce dazzle from other vehicles' lights. Certainly you should dip your lights to avoid dazzling any oncoming traffic, or when you are following other vehicles. If you are being dazzled by someone else's lights, look away from the lights, slow down, and make sure you are capable of stopping easily and safely.

Parking lights
When you are parking in well lit streets at night, there is no need to leave any lights on at all. The use of parking lights can be helpful in some cases, especially if you are parking in badly lit areas, or where you need to draw attention to the fact you have left your car at the kerb side. Don't use your headlights as this is illegal. Even side lights can be quite a drain on your battery and leaving them on too

long could flatten your battery. This can be embarrassing because you'll need help to get started again.

Some cars, (notably Volkswagens), enable you to make use of one side only of your parking lights, by using the indicator switch to the right or left according to which side you are parked. But again you need to remember what the law says about parking at night on the wrong side of the road. It is still an offence to have your lights pointing in the wrong direction. The red light must show to the rear and white to the front – in the direction the traffic flows.

Know the rules for using:

- parking lights.
- main beam.
- dipped beam.
- extra driving lights.
- rear fog-lights.
- hazard-warning lights.

Switch them off when not needed.

The use of lights for signalling is best left to those who think they know what they are doing. Eye contact and a smile is almost always the best way to say thank you. If the people you want to thank are behind you, the best way to say thank you is to get out of their way quickly and safely. Giving unnecessary signals, especially to say thank you, is not only a waste of time, but might distract you from what you should be doing instead. Even worse is the knowledge that signals only mean what the recipient thinks they mean. If the signal is not in the Highway Code, don't use it.

Points to remember

- The importance of clean and clear headlights, and clean indicator lenses too.
- Clean all windows and windscreens often.
- Make sure all your lights work properly, legally, and efficiently.
- Lights must be properly adjusted to avoid dazzling others.
- If dazzled slow down, look away, and prepare to stop.
- Get the maximum benefit from your lights.

- Adjust yourself to driving in the dark.
- Always keep your speed within your visibility.
- Take extra care at dusk and early dawn.
- Compensate for half-light conditions.
- Take even more care in the rain at night.
- Look out for badly illuminated vehicles, cyclists, and pedestrians.
- Expect all other road users to be dim too – anticipate the worst.

NIGHT DRIVING RULES

See and be seen at night

- Always check your lights before you drive;
- Clean the lenses, and carry at least one spare bulb of each type;
- Clean your windscreens – inside and out;
- Use your demisters regularly.

- Use low slung fog-lights, but only in fog and falling snow;
- Use rear fog-lights when visibility is less than 100 metres;
- Use your dipped headlights in bad weather or poor visibility;
- Use additional driving lights (long-range ones) only if they do not dazzle;
- Switch off all fog-lights when they are not needed.

- Carry a torch or hand lamp with you in the car;
- A torch with an amber flashing light is useful too;
- Have a white or reflective coat or arm band in the car – just in case;
- If you break down do not work on the driver's side of the car.

- Don't wear 'night-driving glasses' unless they have prescription lenses;
- The danger time for night driving is just as it is getting dark; stop for a break if necessary, so that you can acclimatize yourself to the dark;
- Give yourself more breaks when driving at night, your eyes tire easily.

- Avoid taking a heavy meal before starting a night drive. It is better to feel hungry than bloated when you are driving long distances.

- If ever you feel drowsy, especially on long motorway runs, get off at the next exit, and walk around the car – if necessary have a snooze before you get back in behind the wheel.

- The time to dip your headlights is just before your main beam reaches the other vehicle. You can hold onto main beam longer on right-hand bends than left ones.

- The time to switch on your lights is just before you wish other people had theirs on too.

- Remember that your lights are needed when your windscreen wipers are used. The more rain the more need there is for being seen by others.

7 Bad-Weather Driving

Bad-weather driving covers a whole range of driving and weather conditions. Rain, whether a light shower or a sudden heavy downpour, can normally be coped with by using wipers, dipped lights, and by driving more carefully. Some bad-weather conditions, such as fog, are much more demanding on your concentration, driving skills, and luck.

Some people manage to learn to drive without ever having to use their windscreen wipers and washers. (Some learn to drive without ever seeing the sun, but that is another story.) There are a few unlucky learners who may have driven in the rain, but have always allowed their instructors to switch on the wipers when they were needed. I remember the driving examiner who once asked a test candidate if she could see all right. Yes, she said. Was she sure, countered the examiner.

'Of course, I read the number plate for you,' she responded.

'But it wasn't raining heavily then,' said the examiner.

'Oh, do you want me to put the wipers on?' she asked him brightly, realization dawning.

'I don't mind at all, but if you don't I shall get out and catch a bus back,' was his terse comment.

When you're on your own you need to know when and how to use all the ancillary controls of your car. It is not just a question of switching on the wipers. You need to know how to adjust the ventilator controls to avoid misting up. Where is the heated rear screen switch? You also need to know how to switch on the rear wiper and washer if you have them fitted. And in some cars you also need a lesson in how to switch them off again.

If all else fails, read the car's instruction book.

You must ensure that your vehicle is in good condition every time you drive. But this is even more essential when the weather turns foul. As you can't be sure when it might rain, you need to know that your tyres always have good tread, that your brakes all work well, wipers and washers are efficient and effective, and that all your lights and indicators work properly, every time you drive. It is not just a question of keeping your tyre tread-depth legal. Each tyre has a footprint of less than the sole of your shoe. If the tread has to displace gallons of water from the road surface every minute, you need a really substantial tread depth to let the water squeeze through. If the front wheels can't displace the water quickly enough there is a danger that they will ride up on the cushion of water and a situation called aquaplaning can arise. The feeling is like floating on air – or water. The only way to cope is to decrease speed – but avoid braking hard – and wait until you can feel the tyres gripping the road again. Braking distances in wet weather are always doubled, and often trebled or more. Keep ten seconds' safety margin between you and the vehicle ahead in any type of bad weather.

See and be seen

The essence of driving in bad weather conditions is to ensure that you can see as clearly as possible, and that all other road users can clearly see you.

Sunshine – as a weather hazard
When the sun shines brightly you're suddenly aware of every smear and scrap of dust on your windscreen and windows. Clean them, inside and out, often, and make sure they are clear of obstructions too. The only obstruction allowed is your tax disc. Lucky mascots and stickers to say you've been everywhere ought to be in the boot, not obstructing your view. Mirrors need cleaning frequently, especially the door ones. And you also need to know how to use your demisters, on both back and front windows. A clean dry cloth is needed to clean your side windows.

Another snag with driving lessons is that they often take place during the day, and you only find out once you have passed your test that an early morning, or late evening, sun can shine directly into your eyes. This is made much worse if the roads are wet, or if the sun is so low on the horizon that it blinds you to all else. It can even be difficult to lower the sun visor enough to block it out without hiding the road ahead as well. If you find this happening you must drive carefully. You cannot drive blithely on into the sunset, without seeing exactly everything that is coming towards you. Similarly when you are fortunate enough to be driving away from the sun, remember that it may affect oncoming drivers who may not be able to see you properly. Allow for them to do something stupid – suddenly.

Using your lights

The need is not only to make sure that you can see, but also that you are seen properly by other road users. This is one of the reasons why you should use your headlights at any time when the weather is dark, dismal, or wet. Dipped headlights are helpful to other road users. Side lights, or parking lights are not much help at all, except when you are parked at the kerbside.

HC 131
Use headlights or front fog lights when visibility is seriously reduced . . . when you cannot see for more than 100 metres (328 ft).

The misuse of front fog-lights causes lots of annoyance. Many vehicles are fitted with extra front fog-lights low down. These must not be used in normal driving conditions, but only in thick fog or falling snow. So don't switch them on simply because it's raining. They will only add to the general dazzle, which makes driving even worse, both for yourself and others.

The same rule applies to rear fog-lights. These too can be a real nuisance if used badly – and it is a motoring offence to use them incorrectly. You should only use these high-intensity lights if visibility is *seriously reduced*. This term, because it is used a lot in the Highway Code, has the meaning shown in the box above: when you cannot see for more than 100 metres. Remember if you have a car following closely behind you rear fog-lights can be a nuisance and a danger. If the vehicle is that close, there is no point in showing additional lights. The only function of rear fog-lights is to let drivers more than 100 metres away know you are there. If this condition is not met switch them off. You will see exactly what I mean on the odd occasions when you follow someone else who is apparently unaware that their rear fog-lights are dazzling those behind.

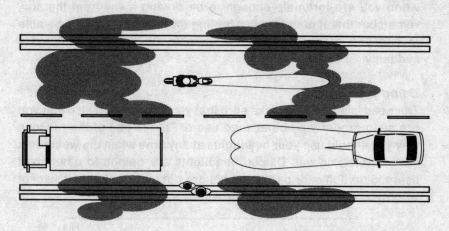

Your speed at night or in fog is limited by your clear visibility. You must be able to stop in the distance you can see to be safe. In fog you cannot rely on other vehicles being properly lit, and they may even be abandoned in the road.

Fog is one of the few weather conditions which puts nearly all the danger out of the hands of the driver. This is why you should avoid driving in the fog if you can. You are so dependent upon the skills and observation powers of other road users that you cannot always guarantee your own safety.

Floods and deep water

If you have to drive through a flooded road, remember that brakes are not very good at all when they are wet. If the wheels have been driven through a ford, or deep water, you will need to dry them out before they can become really efficient again. Disc brakes are less prone to this effect than drum brakes. The car handbook will tell you whether you have disc or drum brakes. Most cars these days have discs at the front and drums to the rear. However, more expensive and sportier cars have discs all round. Only the cheapest of old cars have drum brakes and no servo assistance. You can also tell at a glance if you have discs or drums by looking through or behind the wheels. Discs are nice and shiny and look like dinner plates. Drums are dirty and covered in mud and look like drums.

If you need to dry your brakes after driving through flood water, press your left foot on and off the brake pedal, or keep it pressed down lightly for a short time, whilst still accelerating with the right foot. This should take no more than five or ten seconds, or a hundred metres at the most. Don't look down whilst you are doing it, otherwise you may find a more expensive way of stopping.

Remember too that stopping in wet conditions can take up to four times as long as on dry roads. The natural lubricant for rubber is water. During a long dry spell the tread which has been rubbed off countless thousands of tyres is absorbed into the road surface and produces a nice rubbery surface. A light shower of rain suddenly appearing on this surface doesn't soak in, and it provides an instant skid-pan surface for the unwary.

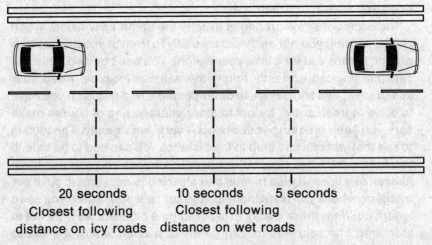

20 seconds
Closest following
distance on icy roads

10 seconds
Closest following
distance on wet roads

5 seconds

Your speed on wet and icy roads is limited by tyre grip on the road surface. You must be able to stop safely in the distance you can do so gently and without locking up the wheels.

Tyre grip depends on three things: the depth and suitability of the tyre tread; the surface of the road; and the speed at which the wheel is turning. The breakaway point comes much sooner if any of these three are suspect. It comes very soon indeed if all three are not suited to the conditions. Skids are never caused by wheels, tyres, ice, or water. Skids are caused by people and by excessive use of brakes, steering, or acceleration for the circumstances at the time. Skids are only ever the result of bad driving. They are dealt with in the section 'Ice and Skids' on p. 90, and in chapter 8.

Snow and ice

Snow is almost easy to deal with. Your biggest advantage is that you can see snow and you know how much room you have in front of you. Unfortunately most people overreact and you should avoid any contact with them. What they do is to realize too late what the problem is and then steer too much the other way, or brake too hard and, as a result, their wheels lock up. That is to say the wheels stop revolving and begin to act like skis. If their front wheels lock up they can't steer.or stop and the car is likely to skid in a straight line. If all four wheels lock they are in dire trouble and totally out of control. Watch out for anyone around you who is moving with locked wheels, and keep well out of their way.

The secret of snow driving is exactly the same as walking. When you're walking you put each foot carefully in front of you and feel the ground before you let it take your weight. You can't quite do this in a car, but you can certainly follow the same principles. Keep your speed slow, and try to drive in other people's tyre marks. If you have to drive in fresh snow, try not to steer sharply, and of course make sure you keep on trying your brakes – very, very gently. The idea is to see that you can still stop in the distance you can see to be safe. If you follow the main run of other people's tracks you can use them like railway lines. It also means that steering is not simple; but if the tracks go where you want them to, this isn't a worry. When you need to turn out from these tracks in order to go a different way, try not to stop first. The secret is to turn gently at a point where the tracks have the lowest edges. If you are in deep ruts you won't be able to get out of them, but if the tracks are simple tyre marks in otherwise fresh snow it is not too difficult to get out. But you must remember that you are now breaking fresh ground yourself. Remember too that you never really know what lies under snow. There might be ice or a hole in the ground. Drive slowly, smoothly and steadily.

Your ability to start and to steer when driving along in snow is much easier when you make easy coaxing movements of your feet and fingers. Use them gently and feel the road through them. Keep in touch with what is happening by feeling through your feet on the pedals. Avoid using the brakes if you can. Feel the road through your fingertips on the steering wheel, they will tell you when your steering seems light – and therefore not working; and through your backside on your seat. You can sense what is happening to the back of your car by a sensation of lightness under your seat. This is what happens when your wheels lock up.

If your wheels do lock up, you will soon be made aware of it by a sliding feeling (your car might even be travelling in a different direction from where your bonnet and wheels are pointing). If this happens you must release the brakes immediately and if you need to brake again, do so gently. If the wheels lock up again, release the brakes once more and keep on repeating the sequence. This is known as pulse or cadence braking. The effect of this is to brake until the wheels are almost locked up. Then you release the brakes in order to be able to steer. This on-off movement with your right foot on the brake pedal avoids some of the problems with skidding. (This is dealt with in detail in chapter 8). Don't make any harsh responses, and avoid locking up your front wheels. If your front wheels are locked, you won't be able to steer and you might not stop either. This is another reason to try your brakes frequently. If you have to drive in snow, keep in the lower gears and allow your engine speed to gradually slow you down when you need to decelerate. Driving in snow needs fingertip precision and the ability to sense your grip on the road surface through your seat and your steering wheel.

Travelling on snow uphill needs a steady start, constant speed and above all no over-revving of the engine. Don't race up and hope to keep going. A slow steady pace is best. Travelling downhill needs the same amount of finesse. Again you need to stay in the lowest suitable gear and avoid touching any of the pedals.

You know that it's illegal to drive at any time with a blocked front or rear window. This applies just as much in snow. You must not try to drive whilst looking through a little porthole in the snow. Clean and clear them before you start off. If the snow continues to fall as you are driving then you may need to stop at intervals to add to the limited range that the wipers sweep. If you do stop, choose a safe, level, and clear place to do so.

Additional snow problems

One incidental danger with snow is that packed snow can pile up around the wheels, and with the front wheels this can affect your steering and brakes too. When you get out to clear your windscreen, knock the snow away from your wheel arches too. You will of course automatically clean your number plate, lights, and indicators so that they can be more easily seen.

An additional problem with snow is that it sometimes covers the road markings. You may know where you are and who has priority on the various roads you are using. If you do know the road, remember that others may not. If you don't know, then assume that you must give way at any time. If in doubt slow right down and expect to stop, just in case the other idiot can't or won't stop.

Ice and skids

Don't take it for granted that if the road is icy you will automatically skid. As with snow, drive slowly, smoothly, and steadily. If you become aware of an icy road, avoid anything which causes sudden changes of speed or direction. Many motorists have driven on icy roads and never even known it. Black ice is often blamed for accidents which are caused by drivers acting stupidly in reaction to something they caused themselves.

Road surfaces do freeze, and in some cases you will find that you have driven onto a section of road that is icy and offering reduced grip to the tyres. It will only affect your driving if you try to change speed or direction more than the road grip allows. Provided you keep straight, and maintain the same slow, steady speed it should not have any effect on your vehicle – or you. If you are driving sensibly, and at a speed at which you can always stop safely, carry on.

This also applies to driving on any rough road surface. Not all roads have a nice tarmac or concrete surface. Loose scree is as bad as ice. Wet tar can be as greasy as ice too on occasions. Always read the road. Look for and cope with whatever road surface you meet.

High winds

High winds have much more effect on high-sided trucks and motorcycles than they do on cars, but even car drivers need to be extra careful when overtaking trucks. Overtaking a truck with a strong sideways wind can have a devastating effect on any car as it suddenly pulls in front. If you expect it you can maintain your grip on the steering wheel to make sure you are not pulled back across or blown further out.

Summary

With all bad-weather conditions the real answer is not to go out in them if you can avoid it. There will be many more dangers out there, because so many other road users do not know how to control themselves and their vehicles properly. Therefore any time you make yourself vulnerable to them, you are more likely to become involved in their confrontations. However, if you do have to drive in bad-weather conditions remember that you do everything you do normally, except you do it more gently and with even less jerks than normally.

Points to remember

- Maintain your vehicle properly at all times.
- Check your tyre treads and pressures regularly.
- Use the controls with extra care, and always smoothly.
- Allow much more room between you and any vehicles ahead.
- Reduce your speed below 50 m.p.h. in aquaplaning conditions.
- Slow down to 20 m.p.h. or less in snow or on ice.
- Never steer and change speed at the same time: only change your speed, faster or slower, on the straight.
- Look for and cope with any road surface or weather conditions.

DRIVING PROCEDURES FOR BAD WEATHER

Before starting your journey

Listen to the weather forecast, and if necessary change your route or your mind. Allocate extra time for the journey and make sure you take suitable clothing (in case you have to get out of the car) and a mobile telephone if you can. Make sure your windows are all clean and clear.

On the road

Use proper lighting to be seen and to see. Remember the dangers of sudden showers on hot, dry roads. Reduce speed to suit the conditions, other traffic and road surfaces. Increase your separation distances.

In fog

Use fog-lights – front and rear – but with courtesy to those around you. Use your demisters, wipers, and washers. Sound your horn if it helps. Turn off your stereo system and beware of fatigue and disorientation. Listen for the sounds of other traffic. Avoid right turns where possible. Also avoid following centre lines and cats' eyes.

In snow and ice

Virgin snow provides adequate grip, but can hide hazards such as deep drifts, pot-holes, or black ice under. Allow much greater distances – as much as twenty or thirty times normal. Use minimum acceleration or braking to avoid wheelspin or skidding. Use your engine power to slow down by deceleration where you can.

General rules

Plan your routes carefully and make sure that someone knows where you are going and what time you expect to arrive. If in doubt, don't go.

8 Skidding

Skidding and skid avoidance training

Most people are almost as scared of the thought of skid training as they are of skidding itself. Even the Driving Standards Agency – which carries out driving tests, and which extols the virtues of additional driver training in its Pass Plus post-test driver-training scheme – advises against letting newly qualified drivers take what it calls 'high-speed skid training'! The Agency falls into the trap that so many people do, of assuming that skid-avoidance training (to give it its proper title) is necessarily carried out at high speed.

The essence of skid training is to enable drivers to recognize the cause of skids, to feel the commencement of a skid, and still be able to get the vehicle back under control, before the driver loses control altogether. This can only be done slowly. It must be taught at slow speeds to give the driver time in which to recognize the stages, identify the causes, and control the effects of the skids which are being created.

> **Skid training enables drivers to recognize the cause of a skid, feel the commencement of it, and learn to regain control. It is done slowly so that the driver is able to recognize the stages building up, identify the cause(s) of each skid, and control the effects of the skid.**

Skid vehicles

Skid training used to take place on skid-pans. These were places the size of a football pitch, with specially prepared road surfaces using grease or oil to prevent the tyres from gripping properly. These days skid-pans have been replaced by skid vehicles, which are cars – and trucks – specially adapted to allow skid simulation to take place. They are very effective, and at the same time totally safe, as the vehicle is always totally under the control of the instructor in the passenger seat. Experienced drivers ought to take at least one skid-training session a year. Newly qualified drivers would benefit even more, as they have everything to learn and nothing to unlearn. They would enjoy it too.

The danger with skid-related accidents – and most road-traffic accidents have skidding as a contributory factor – is that vehicles invariably hit what the driver is looking at. In a skid, drivers find that their feet lock onto the pedals, and their eyes lock onto an object they don't wish to hit; and then they do.

Most drivers' knowledge of skidding is limited to the standard answer to a question they assume driving examiners always ask: 'What do you do in a skid?' Answer: 'Steer into it.' As if this was all there was to know. A useful response to this answer is to ask the supplementary question, 'What do you do if all four wheels are skidding in a straight line heading for a bus?' Steering into the skid is not an option in this case. You must know how to steer away from the skid if all your wheels are locked.

Any form of skid training is much cheaper than any accident claim and certainly more fun. The worry that people often voice is that they don't want to take skid training because they don't know how to do it. Other people use the same excuse not to learn a foreign language because they can't speak it already.

Regardless of the type of skid training you undertake, every driver will learn something. Ideally training should be done every year, not necessarily just before the winter weather conditions are due. Contrary to what you might expect, most skids do not occur on ice. The type of road with the greatest skid potential is any road when there is a light shower of rain after a long, hot, dry spell.

Greasy road conditions

Roads regularly become smothered in a mixture of rubber, dust, and oil. This gunge fills in the natural roughness of the roads making them very smooth. Water is the natural lubricant for rubber and if the water between the tyres and the road cannot escape anywhere, the tyres will suddenly lose their grip. It only needs a light covering of water to produce a perfect skid-pan surface. Once there has been a really heavy downpour of rain, the road surface is washed clean again and the tyres grip as normal.

Drivers need to take skid-avoidance lessons, partly to prevent them from getting complacent, but mainly to remove the fear of skidding. If you're scared of skidding, when it does happen you will freeze on the brakes and you are then committed to hitting whatever is in front of you. If you have had practice – even half an hour a year can be enough – you will know what to do and you will probably be able to steer your way out of trouble, even if you can't brake. Steering (and braking) out of a skid situation is always possible if you know what to do, you have the confidence to do it, and you can unfreeze your feet from the controls.

Skid avoidance

Skidding is illegal, therefore you must know the causes of skids in order to avoid them.

Causes of skidding

- **Skidding occurs when the tyres no longer grip the road surface.**
- **Skidding is caused by excessive use of the brakes, of the steering, or of the accelerator pedal, in relation the speed the car is travelling, and in relation to the grip exerted on the road by the tyres.**
- **Skidding is always caused by the driver's actions.**

In a way it's unfortunate that so many drivers get away with bad driving in skid-potential conditions with nothing going wrong – that particular time. Eventually when an accident does occur they can see nothing in their driving which could have caused it. Because they always drive that way, they assume someone or something else caused the skid and the resultant accident. It was nothing to do with them, they just drove as they normally do.

Avoiding skidding

- **The first way to avoid skidding is by making sure that you always have good, equal, and substantial tread on each of your tyres.**
- **The second way is driving slowly enough to be able to brake to a stop easily in the distance you can see to be safe.**
- **Knowing how to avoid skidding is the life saver, and is much more important than knowing what to do when the skid occurs.**

Quick reactions to skids

Skid training explains how skids are caused, and how they can be avoided. Secondly, it teaches the skills needed for instant recognition not only of the type of skid but the underlying cause of that particular skid. The third stage of skid training is to know how to undo the cause.

The obvious way to recover from a skid is to stop doing what caused it. If it's caused by excessive braking, come off the brakes. If it's caused by excessive acceleration, come off the gas. If it's caused by steering too harshly, get your wheels straight again – even if this means aiming initially where you don't want to go. If it's a combination of errors, correct them all as soon as possible.

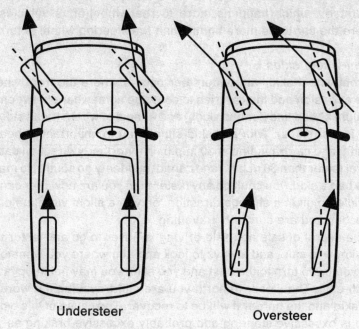

Understeer   Oversteer

Understeer means your car turns in a wider radius than where the wheels are pointing. Oversteer means your car turns more sharply than where the wheels are pointing.

slip angle

Skidding occurs when your tyres lose their grip and travel in a wrong direction - the greater the slip angle, the worse the skid.

Apart from running into the back of the car in front, the two most common types of skid, front- and rear-wheel skids, take place on corners, when the driver wants the car to follow a bend and the car doesn't. As well as the loss of tyre grip on the bend there are two added factors which need to be taken into account. They are called *understeer* and *oversteer*. A certain amount of understeer is built into most front-wheel-drive cars. The car doesn't seem to turn as much as the driver's movements on the steering wheel intended.

Oversteer, which happens more to rear-wheel-drive vehicles, is where the car turns more tightly than the steering wheel is turned.

Front-wheel skids
A front-wheel skid with understeer occurs where the front wheels lose adhesion and the car tries to continue somewhere between the straight ahead line (for bad skids) and almost to where it was steered (for lesser skids). With any skid situation it is important to bear in mind that a car travelling at 30 m.p.h. in a northerly direction cannot travel faster than 30 m.p.h., and cannot suddenly go south. No matter how bad a skid, you can't go any faster than you are now. Nor can the vehicle go off in a strange direction, only in a slight variation of the direction you are currently travelling.

The secret of safe non-skid driving is never to go any faster than you know is safe, and always to look and aim where you want to go.

If you try to turn to the east and you skid, you may finish up facing north-east. The closer to north you are still travelling the worse is the skid and the harder it will be to recover. The cause of this type of skid is excessive steering and probably excessive braking as well for the road surface and tyre conditions which exist.

Reduce speed by deceleration, *not* by braking, and steer back into the direction the car is still travelling. When grip has been restored, try to steer again in the way you wish to go, with more care, and at a lower speed. Irrespective of any mechanical or climatic cause of the skid – excessive steering and speed – the real reason is always driver error.

Rear-wheel skids
In an oversteer, the slip angle of the rear tyres exceeds that of the front tyres. Again this can be caused by excessive speed coupled with excessive steering once again. This skid can also be induced by suddenly coming off the accelerator, or braking, halfway round a corner. If the brakes are applied, or the steering angle increased at the same time, a classic rear-wheel skid will almost always ensue. The rear-wheel skid develops when the rear of the car goes faster than, and starts to overtake, the front of it.

It is this condition to which the classic answer 'Steer into the skid' really does apply. If the rear is moving out to the right as a result of trying to steer to the left, then the correct action is to steer back to the right again, but only for a moment. This must be done to regain control, before trying the turn once again – this time slower and with less oversteer action. The weakness of this particular advice, however, is that quite often the steering into the skid action takes place too late, and too fiercely. Consequently a pendulum effect begins. Controlling or correcting this is even more difficult and often never happens.

Four-wheel skids

These are the result of losing your grip with all four tyres. The basic cause – in a straight line – is almost always excessive braking for the road surface grip available. Where it takes place on a corner, the cause is almost certainly excessive speed for the change of direction wanted. If the road is dry with the brakes locked hard on, this is definitely the cause.

Pulse and cadence braking

Once the wheels are locked up you have a dilemma. Do you keep the brakes locked hard on and pray that something positive may happen? Or do you release the brakes, hoping that the wheels will start revolving again, knowing that you don't really want the wheels to revolve, you want them to stop the car from travelling forward? You will only ever have to brake hard in an emergency anyway; so getting your wheels locked up in an emergency merely exacerbates the situation. The answer is to use either *pulse* or *cadence* braking. This is a better method of stopping – in a real emergency.

   The object is to brake fairly hard, but not so hard that the front wheels stop turning. Then you release the brakes so that you can still steer. Then you have to brake again. The methods of operation of pulse and cadence braking are slightly different, but with the same objectives. In *pulse* braking the idea is to rapidly hit the footbrake and release it – braking in short sharp pulses. The purpose behind this is to avoid getting the front wheels to bite harshly into the ground – because this would automatically make the back end of the car lift away from the ground and reduce the rear wheel braking effort. In *cadence* braking the periods of time spent braking are longer. The objective here is to transfer the weight onto the front wheels in a rhythmical fashion, then release the brakes so that maximum steering effort is available when there is the maximum grip on the front tyres.

Pulse braking works like this: Brake, ease off. Brake, ease off. Brake, ease off. Brake, ease off. Keep on doing this until your speed has dropped sufficiently to enable you to continue braking to a stop.

Cadence braking takes longer – like this: Brake, keep braking until you can sense lock up – then ease off and steer. Brake, keep braking until you can sense lock up, then ease off and steer. Brake, keep on braking – and maybe this time your wheels won't lock up. Then you can steer safely out of the problem.

Choosing the best method is not something you do after a great deal of discussion and thought. If the need is to steer – and steer quickly – then cadence braking will enable you to slow down a bit whilst you are braking, and to steer a little bit whilst you are not braking. On the other hand, if the object is to stop quickly in a straight line, pulse braking is better for this. But as I said you don't normally have time to think about it. You need to react – IMMEDIATELY! This is why skid-pan or skid vehicle training is so necessary. You need to train your reactions to cope with what you can see – and to identify immediately where you need to go and what you want to avoid hitting. Practice under controlled conditions is essential – and can also be good fun.

ABS and Traction Control Systems
Traction Control Systems are a fairly recent innovation. Many new and more expensive cars are fitted with some form of traction control. The idea of this is that each wheel has sensors attached to it so that should any of the tyres lose their grip when the car is driving in greasy or icy conditions, the others compensate for it. The wheels which have lost their grip won't spin. This enables you to keep full control over two or three of the wheels even if one or two of them have lost their grip.

On the other hand you may drive a car fitted with ABS (Anti-lock Braking Systems) which does the same thing for you almost as effectively. If your car is fitted with ABS (and many newer, more expensive, ones do have them these days), then you may suddenly get this rattling feeling from the front end when you are braking harshly. This is the ABS taking over. Use it as an example. It is telling you that you were driving too fast on that occasion. Don't do it again. ABS is not foolproof, and is certainly not idiot-proof.

> **ABS braking allows you to brake and steer at the same time. But this is only as a last resort, and not something you should ever plan to do. ABS does not enable you to stop more quickly. ABS is not a device to enable you to drive round bends faster than normal, and yet still manage to steer. ABS is a safety feature fitted to save idiots – but not always – from their own lack of skill and over-exuberance.**

Correct driving

Driving through bends should always follow the pattern of entering slowly, using gentle acceleration through, and increasing acceleration out. Never try to brake and steer at the same time. Braking prevents the wheels from turning, steering needs the wheels to revolve in order to steer.

It is worthwhile remembering that many years ago, when rear-wheel drive, cross-ply tyres, and all-drum brakes were the norm, drivers had to enter bends in the wet very slowly or else they did not survive. Today drivers are cossetted by better designed cars, radial tyres, ABS, TCS, and disc brakes. However the invention of various safety devices must never encourage you to take risks, but possibly act as a safety net if you forget.

Points to remember

- Skidding is illegal – never practise on any public roads.
- Skid *avoidance* training is an essential lesson for every driver.
- Skids are caused by the nut holding the wheel.

- Skids would never occur if drivers looked and planned further ahead.
- In a *front-wheel skid* feet off pedals and steer where the car is going – then steer where you want to go – under control.
- In a *rear-wheel skid* steer towards the way you were going – then steer gently to where you want to go.
- In a *four-wheel skid*, pulse or cadence brake in order to slow – then brake and steer around the danger ahead.
- Excessive speed is always a strong contributory factor in skidding.
- If you are in a skid, remember to *look* where you want to go.

Skid Recognition, Identification, and Control

Type of Skid	Cause	Remedy
Front-wheel	Braking too hard, which prevents steering.	Come off the brake, line the front wheels up in the direction you are travelling until steering control is regained. Then try to steer where you want to go.
Rear-wheel	Turning too hard into a bend.	Steer back in the way the car wants to go, lose speed, and try to turn correctly again.
Four-wheel	Harsh braking at too high a speed.	Off brakes; pulse brake if you know how. Steer to avoid collision, if you can. Brake without locking up if you are able.
Other skid effects	Burst tyre: Front:	Hold the steering wheel very firmly; aim where you want to go. If you are on a motorway steer gently towards the left.
	Rear:	Hold the wheel steady, pulse brake *gently* to transfer the weight to the front of the car.
Aquaplaning	Excessive speed on wet roads.	Although this doesn't obviously fit into the normal skid pattern, the effect is that you are riding high on a wedge of water. Braking and steering will not work until your speed is decreased and the front wheels are gripping again. Decelerate and wait until your steering wheels are in contact with the road again. Avoid turning the steering wheel whilst aquaplaning.

Skidding is always caused by driver error

9 Advanced Driving

What is advanced driving?

Two or three years ago the Department of Transport called together all the experts in the business of 'Advanced driving, training and testing' in order to standardize advanced testing and training nationally. It was then found that there wasn't a recognized definition for what advanced really meant. So for three consecutive monthly meetings, about twelve of the country's top 'advanced' driving exponents sat around a table trying to define what we ourselves meant by 'advanced'. At the end of the third meeting we were no further forward. Each advanced testing organization, and there are three major ones, had its own view; and amongst the advanced driver trainers there was just as much variation.

'Everyone knows what it is, but they may not be able to define it,' was the sort of statement that emanated from some quarters. 'Being better than you were,' was my own offering. Others felt that it could be called 'Thinking', 'Safer', 'Considerate' or 'Planned Driving'.

Advanced driving has suffered in many ways in that there have historically been artificial barriers built between Department of Transport standards, which have apparently only been concerned with the L test, and the police driving standards, based around the book *Roadcraft*. Other distractions have arisen through the term Approved Driving Instructor being interpreted as an Advanced Driving Instructor. However advanced driving exists; and although there have been less than half a million drivers (out of more than thirty million) who have taken advanced driving tests in the past forty years the concept is still acceptable and many drivers are prepared to look with awe on anyone whose car displays any form of advanced badging.

How can you aspire to being an advanced driver?

Hazard procedure

Anything which causes a driver to change speed or direction, or anything which makes them think about changing speed or direction, comes under the heading of a hazard. There is a set procedure which you must always follow, and which you can recognize as the safest possible sequence to follow. It is quite simple, and one that you undoubtedly put into operation when you are concentrating on your driving. The problem is that we do not always put it into operation when we are thinking about something else, and our driving is on autopilot. Therefore it's essential to practise this form of hazard procedure so that even when you're not concentrating on the road ahead as much as you should, you're still conditioned to apply this sequence immediately a hazard begins.

First of all you must always plan your driving well ahead, and rather than thinking of a set distance in front of you, regard it as seconds in time. You must never be thinking less than five to ten seconds ahead of yourself, because this is the greatest single cause of traffic accidents. You will know the 'two-second' rule, that says your vehicle must never be closer than two seconds' travel from the vehicle ahead of you. If you pass an object on the road less than two seconds after the vehicle did, then no matter what else happens, the decision whether you run into the back of that vehicle is taken completely out of your hands. If you maintain a distance of more than two seconds (much more if the roads are wet or greasy), and you are planning your driving at least five seconds ahead, you should be in a position to stop safely provided you are concentrating ahead and only thinking of your driving. If your brain is elsewhere or your attention is less than ten seconds ahead you will still have problems stopping safely.

The ideal advanced driving hazard procedure takes into account the obvious facts that observation and action take place simultaneously, and that drivers need to make continuous adjustments to speed and position with regard to what is happening ahead, around, and behind them.

> ## The Observation and Information stage
> (which lasts throughout the sequence)
>
> ## Position   Speed   Gear   Acceleration
> (which is the practical application)

The observation and information stage

This is the single most important item because it concerns what is happening outside the vehicle, and it consists of three separate components: *what information* is received by the driver; *how the information* is understood; and *what information* is given by the driver to other road users.

The action sequence, the one that becomes part of each advanced driver's automatic response to any situation, is to: position the vehicle on the *safety line* at all times; drive at the *speed* at which it is easy to stop safely; use the most suitable *gear* for the action to be completed.

Only then can *acceleration* be applied.

Information is gained through observation and awareness. It is given by signals and positioning. Information is gathered in many ways; the most important for a driver is through the eyes. We assimilate more than 75% of all our information visually: 17% is gained aurally, and the remainder through taste, touch, smell, and kinaesthesis. The last one sounds highly technical, but simply refers to the awareness of successful muscular effort that accompanies any voluntary motion made by any person. It is the means by which skilful operators receive feedback through a combination of 'awareness and touch' to confirm their recognition of how well each physical task has been accomplished.

Use of mirrors

In a motor car the driver sits looking through the windscreen with occasional glances through the various mirrors, and with rarer looks over either shoulder to cover blind spots. Virtually all of the driver's awareness of road and traffic conditions is therefore received by the eyes from what is happening ahead. Advanced drivers would like to think that their use of mirrors is greater than that of other road users. It is not just a question of using the mirrors more often, but taking greater account of everything that is seen.

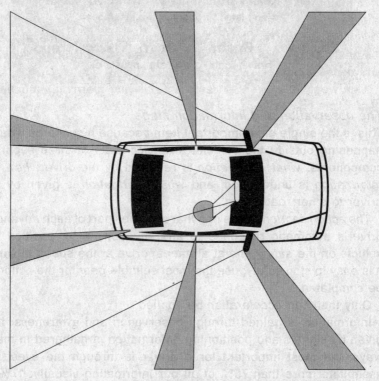

Beware of blind spots (the grey areas) when using your mirrors. Move your head and look all round when necessary.

Many drivers have taken on board their memories of L-driver training and will even be able to quote the phrase 'mirrors, signal, and manoeuvre' quite easily. But quite often their understanding of proper use of their mirrors has become dimmed with time and usage. One of the most notable things that advanced driving instructors notice about other drivers' use of mirrors is how little genuine information actually gets through to the driver.

To obtain the maximum benefit from information available it is necessary to carry out full mirror searches. The mirrors must be regarded as extensions to the windscreen. Mirrors are a means of extending the driver's ability to see around without moving the head any more than is necessary. Mirrors are the third eye; they enable drivers to avoid being taken by surprise by whatever is happening behind and alongside them. On a motorway where all the traffic in a lane is driving at almost the same speed, the use of mirrors can be minimal. But in residential areas, or in heavy traffic where the differences in speed of the various vehicles are apparent, then constant and correct mirror use becomes an essential aid to all planning and decision making. *Look often, see all, filter out what is not necessary.*

One weakness of M-S-M as a safe driving learning sequence is that it can so easily relegate the use of mirrors to a simple, once only check before a driver commences a turning or changes speed. Drivers say to themselves that they have checked their mirror (note the singular use), therefore it's safe to do whatever it is that comes next. This is also where good motorcyclists have the edge on most car drivers. They dare not forget the use of what they rightly consider their final 'life-saver look' in the mirrors, and another look over their shoulder whenever they intend to turn right.

Proper use of the mirrors is part of every advanced driver's thinking and planning philosophy. The best way to plan properly is to ask yourself pertinent and relevant questions. The answers which you give to yourself must then be used in relation to the situation which exists at the moment, coupled to its potential for change. The questions are simple ones:

- **What changes of speed or position am I likely to make in the next five to fifteen seconds?**
- **What effect could these changes have on other road users?**
- **Who, and where, are these other road users?**
- **What can I tell them to make things safer for everyone?**

These are then followed by this one statement of intent:

- **Give a sensible and recognizable signal to anyone who may benefit!**

'Full observation' has been defined as a total awareness of everything all around you at any particular time. On long, straight journeys your awareness will be fairly high, even though changes occur relatively rarely. In busy residential and urban shopping areas it is impossible to know *all* that is happening around you, and your observation must always be selective. In order to be safe you need to identify what is important, and what you need to look for. You also need to learn how to filter out material which is not needed, and which can be ignored with safety. Once you are aware of the whole traffic situation, you are also able to make positive decisions with regard to telling others.

Giving signals

Signals should always be given as a result of thought, and not made out of habit. Once again the theory of M-S-M from learner-driver days is brought home. A signal *must* be given if anyone, anywhere, might benefit. The snag is that a signal is so often needed for turning left and right that many drivers give it as a matter of course. The signal then fails to be a mental decision but just a mechanical and digital one. A conscious signal must mean something specific. And someone will probably appreciate exactly what is meant. Eye contact with that road user will make it even more effective.

Signals are normally given by indicators, positioning, and brake lights, but there are some occasions when an arm signal can have greater significance. Slowing-down arm signals, combined with eye contact, benefit pedestrians who are waiting at crossings more than anything else ever can. And of course the position that a vehicle takes up in the road gives the strongest clues to what is intended. Unfortunately many motorists themselves rely on other road users' positions and actions so much they do not see the need to give intelligent signals themselves.

A signal given late can often be almost useless. The idea of giving the signal is to ensure that other road users get the maximum warning of your intentions. Information is the key to your safety. What you see tells you what you can do and what you tell others explains (but never demands) what your intentions are.

Information must be recognized for what it really is – a vital part of a two-way communication system. Observation enables available information to be an aid to safer driving for all road users.

The action sequence

This takes place throughout the information stage.

Position
Taking up the correct position is essential, and just as important is the need to adopt the correct position early enough so that as little inconvenience as possible is caused to other road users. Correct positioning can actually help others to remain safe too.

Once the mirrors and signals have been used effectively, advanced drivers are able to move quickly and safely to a position which can be maintained safely throughout the whole manoeuvre. While driving straight ahead and turning to the left, this normal position should either be central in the chosen lane, or at a distance from the kerb of about one metre. Most lanes allow a normal car to be centred in the lane, and about one metre from each painted line. Naturally if there are any obstructions on the left, then the safety line follows a path which allows one metre from that obstruction. Before moving out for these obstructions the full information sequence of observation and signal if necessary must be used.

Speed
The correct speed is easy to define. An advanced driver chooses the most *suitable* speed for the situation. This must take into account the need always to be able to stop safely in the distance which can be seen to be safe. Other factors include speed limits, comfort of passengers, care for other road users, and the purpose of the journey. This is not to say that the correct speed is always the fastest possible which is still safe. On all normal driving occasions it is advisable to travel slower than the maximum possible. Fuel consumption is one reason; wear and tear on the vehicle a second; the need to enjoy the journey is another. Therefore the choice of the optimum speed takes into account every factor about the journey. Although these factors include: the reason for the journey; the time that journey will take; the comfort, safety, and considerations of all passengers; the strain and stress on the vehicle; the road and traffic constraints; any speed limits in force; and the relaxation of the driver him- or herself; the overall safety factor must predominate.

There are two final points about speed which are so obvious they are often overlooked. First, the urgency of the time of arrival should never be a factor. You can always arrive early if you start early. If you are late leaving, you will be late arriving. Always allow plenty of time for your journey. Secondly, there are two speeds which need to be considered: the speed at which a vehicle is travelling in relation to the road conditions, and the speed of the vehicle in relation to the traffic flow. Both must always be proportionate to the conditions.

Gear

Choice of gear is much more personal. Once more the comfort factor is important. In all cases the most *suitable* gear should be selected. This again depends on the answers to a series of questions you need to ask yourself.

- Is the intention to go slower, faster, or maintain this speed?
- Does the road ahead go uphill or downhill?
- What is the road surface?
- What sort of tyre grip exists?
- What is the other traffic doing?
- What sort of vehicle am I driving?
- What acceleration potential does it have?

The choice of gear finally depends on the experience of the driver in relation to the vehicle being driven, the road and traffic conditions which are being faced, and the purpose of the journey.

Other questions which concern you are to do with other drivers and road users, and in a way may be even more important.

- Why is this driver so slow?
- Is there a reason why they are dawdling?
- Why is this driver so fast?
- Could they have a genuine reason for getting past me?
- What can I do to keep out of their way?

Acceleration

This is always emotive. According to the dictionary 'accelerator' means a device to make something go quicker. It even refers to it as the pedal for *increasing* the speed of a motor engine. However, using the accelerator can refer to the *steady* use of the pedal in order to maintain a set engine speed, rather than continuing to increase speed.

In this safe driving sequence sense it only refers to the use of the pedal. The control of the accelerator is very much dependent upon the vehicle and how it matches each driver's own abilities and capabilities. The skill of acceleration shows itself in the way the vehicle handles, and can be measured easily by a passenger's comfort. Excessive acceleration uses excessive fuel, increases tyre wear, and can easily upset other road users.

Intelligent acceleration is always the safe and smooth option.

Throughout the whole of the driving system there is only one way to regard acceleration – any acceleration which is followed immediately by braking is not only a waste of fuel, it is a sign of lack of anticipation and awareness. This fault is the root cause of most driving accidents. It is a sign of impatience and aggressive driving.

Observation

Throughout the whole of the driving system observation is paramount. This is why it can no longer be regarded as one separate and individual item slotted in between the other 'in-car' actions. Observation – proper observation – takes place throughout the whole of every driving operation. Drivers need to spend the whole of the time they are driving looking ahead, keeping track of what is in their mirrors, and planning what to do in the next five, ten, and fifteen seconds.

Remember that your next two to four seconds have already been planned and commitments made. Any change to this is panic.

Driving on *permanent* autopilot is not part of any advanced driver's safe routine. In the early part of this book I commented on the fact that you can recognise when a driver improves beyond the 'competent' stage of the ex-learner driver to become proficient, by noting that they are able to go into autopilot stage quite easily. The reason for this is easy to see. When you are learning to drive, and even whilst you are driving for a while after the test, everything that you do is the result of a conscious effort and decision. Then one day you arrive at your destination without being consciously aware of making any gear change decisions. Fairly soon after that you are able to drive without consciously reacting to traffic lights or the brake lights of the vehicles ahead of you. You are driving on autopilot and have now reached a stage of proficiency which you never dreamed possible as a learner driver.

Unfortunately some people never get beyond this stage. This is the sum total of their driving ability. These are the drivers I referred to right at the beginning of this book – those who do not learn from experience, and who, sadly, are no safer now than in the year in which they took their driving tests. In order to get beyond the stages of competence and proficiency which can lead on to advanced driving, these drivers need to go through the third stage of 'expertise' which lifts them out of the rut of being average drivers.

Their driving is always on autopilot, and their thoughts and attention are locked firmly onto anything except their driving. The object of this book is to make ordinary drivers realise that they are capable of driving to the highest standards provided they concentrate on what they need to do. The difference between a good driver and an average driver is that the good driver concentrates on the driving task for longer periods of time; and is more aware of what is happening all the time.

In order to be an expert driver you must know when you can use your autopilot system as a break, and when you need to get out of autopilot and take instant charge again.

The way to recognise this, and to use it to your advantage, is to recognise that every journey is different. Each day's traffic presents new dangers, and every road user has a different approach to what is happening. The reason for this, even when you are travelling on the same route, at the same time, and with apparently the same vehicles on a daily journey, is that the people around you are different. They may react differently today from the way they reacted yesterday. By watching others, by looking for tell-tale warnings of change, and by expecting the unexpected, you can lift yourself out of the ordinary and become an expert driver, quite simply.

If you continue to drive on autopilot because you believe you can cope without thinking – automatically – with any sudden change, you have become an 'ordinary' driver again. Ordinary drivers are those who, statistically, have a minor accident every year, and a serious or fatal one every twenty years or so. Truly advanced drivers never drive on autopilot, they prefer to plan – and live. Advanced drivers take everyone else's actions into account as well as their own, and ensure that they are never taken by surprise.

Safe driving is no accident
A guaranteed safe arrival at the end of every journey is the result of planning and putting into practice safe-driving principles the whole of the time spent behind the wheel. That is what is meant by systematic driving. What is needed is a kinaesthetic system of safe-driving principles which enables your body and brain to recognize when you are driving well, a system which allows you to concentrate on your driving task, and to plan and put into operation each of the elements of the system – safely, success-fully, and without any apparent effort.

The only way to do this is to ensure that each stage of the system is practised each time you drive.

Advanced driving is safe driving

- Always take up the correct position – that is to follow your safety line.
- Keep your speed slow enough to match your safe following distance.
- Look as far ahead as you can in order to plan your driving effectively.
- Use your mirrors, all of them, to be fully aware of what is behind and around you.
- Give whatever signals you need so that no one is in any doubt.
- Only change your position after you have seen, signalled, and confirmed.
- Brake or decelerate only once for each hazard.
- Change gear only once for each hazard – skipping gears if necessary.
- When you see the road ahead is clear, accelerate out from the hazard.
- Expect all other road users to do the unexpected and give them room.

Advanced driving tests

People take advanced driving tests for a number of reasons: because they like the idea of a badge on the front of their car or on their jacket, or so they can wear a special tie or scarf with the logo on it which tells those who are interested of the additional skills of the wearer; others take them to prove to themselves that they are safer than other drivers and less likely to have an accident. These days a number of drivers take the tests because their employers want them to, or as a result of taking a training course in advanced driving to validate what they have learned. A considerable number of drivers take advanced driving tests in the hope of gaining increased insurance cover for a smaller premium. More and more insurance companies endorse the benefit of further driver training, and these days many company cars can only be covered for business use at reasonable insurance rates, or with acceptable excess payments, if the drivers have taken an approved course of driver training. The only way to measure the eventual effectiveness of that training is in the reduction of accidents and damage; but as a temporary form of validation, an independent examination of driving skills at advanced levels is ideal.

Company driver training and testing
In the present day world of driver training, with fewer learner drivers needing to take L tests, the only growth market is corporate training. Company drivers can reduce their accident rates by up to 90%, they can reduce wear and tear on their vehicles by more than 30% and they can improve their fuel efficiency by over 15% every year. This latter figure can be achieved easily by any driver who is shown how to drive their car following a simple system of planned driving. Yet this same figure is the equivalent of not paying your vehicle fuel bills in January and February every year. This represents sums of up to £500,000 annually for many of Britain's bigger corporate businesses. It is small wonder that so many of them are now getting their drivers trained to drive to a safe-driving system. Accidents which do not happen are hard to identify, wear and tear on vehicles is also difficult to quantify; but everyone can recognize the value of not paying one sixth of their annual fuel bills. An

average business driver who spends about £150 per month on petrol or diesel can easily save £300 per year or more, simply by adopting a fresh approach to driving. Advanced training and advanced driving tests can be had for much less than £300 per driver per year.

The IAM Advanced Driving Test

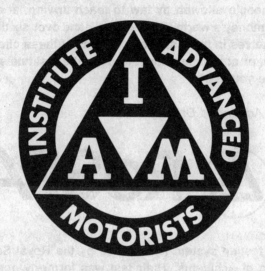

The Institute of Advanced Motorists (IAM) is probably the best known of the various advanced driving tests which can be taken. Its badge is a red triangle which proclaims the driver's skill and it can be fitted with a little plastic cover to be used when the driver is not at the wheel. The test itself can be taken in most areas of the country, with one of the Institute's two hundred and fifty appointed examiners. Commentary driving used to be asked for, but these days it is always an option. Give a commentary if you wish, but remember that the examiner probably knows even better than you do why you are about to do the action that follows.

All IAM examiners are holders of a Police Advanced Driving Certificate. Most of them are serving officers and some are retired. They will conduct tests at times and places to suit the applicant. In preparing to take the test you will be offered the option of joining one of their local groups for a small fee in order to have your driving assessed and if necessary raised to the IAM's standards. Some of the IAM's Trainers and Assessors are either Advanced Driving Intructors (ADIs) or hold an Advanced Police Drivers Instructors' Certificate, or an Advanced Police Drivers Certificate. However, others who may do the assessing and some of the training are not driving instructors and may have very little skill in assessing and teaching. It's better to get professional training from a Government Approved Driving Instructor, who are the only people allowed by law to teach driving, at any level, for money or money's worth. On the other hand over six thousand ADIs are themselves in the Institute and many of these offer training for no charge, or at reduced rates, through the Institute's own groups. Ask before you start.

RoSPA's Advanced Driving Test

A similar testing system is operated by the Royal Society for the Prevention of Accidents. Their test was formerly operated by the League of Safe Drivers, and their badge is a distinctive green star with a centre boss of gold, silver, or bronze, showing that you are a Grade 1, 2, or 3 advanced driver. This is one of the differences between the two tests: the RoSPA test result is given as a grading, rather than the straight pass or fail offered by the IAM. The other difference is that RoSPA require their advanced drivers to retake their driving test every three years if they graded 1 or 2, and within twelve months if they only achieve a bronze grade 3 pass.

The IAM test can also be taken again at intervals, if you wish, in order to confirm that you still maintain the standards you achieved when you passed. Indeed many of the IAM and RoSPA examiners conduct tests for both organizations, and in some areas of the country their separate local groups meet and discuss driving matters together. The IAM employs mainly serving and some retired advanced police drivers as its examiners, whilst the RoSPA takes on serving officers as part-time examiners. The IAM is by far the larger of the two organizations and has carried out over a third of a million tests since it was formed in 1956. This is not such a lot compared with the fifty million drivers who have held driving licences since that date, and those who do pass their advanced driving tests can indeed identify themselves as belonging to the top five per cent of safe drivers in the country.

How the driving is tested

Both require candidates to follow the format used in the police 'method' or system of driving as published since 1955 in the HMSO handbook *Roadcraft*. The general public are not required to reach the same standard as police drivers, however. For many years devotees and students of *Roadcraft* have found it difficult to comprehend without the reinforcement of police style training, and the length of time needed to take it all in. Whilst it was easy to understand when presented as part of a practical training course, it led to problems when drivers read the book for themselves without the benefit of the additional practical expertise of the police instructors. *Roadcraft* presented a 'System' of car control which was ideal, provided you realised that each item had to be considered rather than implemented as a matter of course. The 'System' advocated a sequence of operation considerably more involved than that used by the Department of Transport in its own publication *Driving*. However in recent years even the police driving schools have seen merit in changing some of the more rigid rules they applied over the years. The insistence on never crossing hands on the steering wheel, the abhorrence of simultaneous braking and gear changing, and for some even the use of block gear changing (missing out intermediate gears when braking) were all absolute rules never to be broken. After considerable discussion, some of which the author was party to, a new rewrite of *Roadcraft* was eventually agreed after considerable and heated argument by some of the older stalwarts of the original system.

The new system which is acceptable to all advanced examiners is now the same as that shown earlier in this book. There are two actual sequences. One is concerned with observation and receiving and giving information. The second is concerned with the mechanical operation of the controls. Drivers need to take up the correct position, adjust their speed to suit their requirements, and then select the gear that is needed. Adherents to this system, and those who follow the advice given in this book, will pass any advanced driving test.

The IAM and RoSPA examiners look at the whole picture presented by the driver, examining each of the precepts laid down.

- **The application of the system of car control;**
- **Acceleration, gear changing, braking, and steering;**
- **Observation and anticipation;**
- **Positioning, cornering, and signalling;**
- **Overtaking, making progress with safety;**
- **Manoeuvrability, consideration for other road users;**
- **Familiarity with the vehicle.**

Both tests last about ninety minutes and involve meeting the examiner in a prearranged venue, quite often a public car park. The tests begin with the examiner asking a few questions about yourself and your vehicle. This is followed by an explanation of how the test will be conducted. The test will cover most types of roads, but especially allows use of national speed limits. Obviously speed restrictions must be obeyed at all times, but it is worth mentioning the way that all driving examiners, not just advanced ones, regard the speedometer of a motor car whilst conducting a driving test. Whilst an examiner is conducting a test he is advised to watch the road ahead and what the candidate is doing. Under normal circumstances he will not need to glance at the car's speedometer unless and until the driver's actions suggest to him that he ought to know the actual speed the car is travelling. This could be because the driver is too slow or because the car is too close to vehicles ahead. If nothing causes the examiner to look, there is no reason why he should. On the other hand the law does enforce speed limits for a purpose and if you are caught breaking the speed limit, either by a following police vehicle or by radar or photographs, then you must accept the consequences.

Breaking any speed limit, on conviction in court or as a fixed penalty, will bring with it an automatic penalty point award of between three and six penalty points. Can you afford to have any penalty points at all? The answer must be no. Apart from any automatic ban and loss of licence if the penalty points reach twelve, the fact that you are speeding alone means you are a danger to yourself and others.

The DIAmond Advanced Driving Test

This is the last of the three national advanced driving tests. The spelling of DIA-mond identifies its origin, as it was produced three or four years ago by the Driving Instructors' Association in response to calls from many new drivers and professional driving instructors who wanted an advanced driving test which continued the logical pattern after taking and passing the basic government L-test.

It differs in two ways from the other two advanced driving tests. Both of the others conduct a highly subjective driving test with examiners who are undoubtedly drivers of very high standards. The DIAmond Advanced Driving Test is based on the Department of Transport and the *Driving Manual* guidelines. The actual standard required of candidates is exactly the same as that required for the second stage of the Approved Driving Instructors examination. Anyone who passes this test not only knows they are good and safe drivers, they also know exactly what standard is required of them.

The ordinary L test is marked subjectively by driving examiners employed by the Driving Standards Agency but to objective and precise standards. Driving which would earn a pass in any part of the country would gain a pass anywhere else. Driving examiners are trained very thoroughly, and certainly much more so than the advanced examiners of the IAM and RoSPA, in standardized driving and examining techniques. These objective standards required of an L driver are simple. Candidates must not make any serious or dangerous errors: serious errors are defined as those that do or might involve other road users, causing them to brake or change direction, and dangerous ones are defined as those which involve actual danger and may even require the examiner to take some form of avoiding action. However there is a third – less important – type of error which is recorded and these are classified as of minor importance. They are recognized as departures from the high standard of a perfect drive, but insufficiently important to state that the candidate is not a competent driver.

If you wanted to become a professional driving instructor, or an examiner, you would take an almost identical test (it lasts a lot longer and obviously covers much greater mileage) but the number of minor errors you are allowed to make is limited (in the case of professional Approved Driving Instructors) to six minor faults in one hour's driving. This is the same standard laid down by the DIAmond Advanced Driving Test organization for its advanced test. Candidates are also required to take some form of professional training before they can apply to take the test and must obtain the signature of an Approved Driving Instructor to say they are likely to pass and they have taken a suitable course of training. Preparation for the two other tests can be given, and often is, by other drivers who have passed that level of driving, but do not necessarily have any training in teaching skills.

Readers who may wish to take any of the advanced driving tests are invited to take all three. There is a definite difference in standards required, though no doubt supporters of each of the three tests would argue that their own particular favourite has the highest standard. However, many senior administrators in these organizations would agree that the DIAmond test does have the most rigid degree of supervision and control of standards. All DIAmond examiners are constantly supervised to Driving Standards Agency levels of competence, and the supervision is carried out by a former Department of Transport Deputy Chief Driving Examiner.

The Cardington A Driving Test

DIAmond Advanced examiners are all professional driving teachers who have passed the Associated Examining Board's Diploma in Driving Instruction, the Cardington A Driving Test, and have taken a stringent course of training by former DSA staff in advanced driver testing techniques. The Cardington driving test is unique in the world of advanced driving tests. Cardington, near Bedford, has been the home of Government Driver Training since 1976 when it moved from its previous home near Heathrow Airport. All driving examiners are trained there, and since 1976 professional driving instructors have been invited to take what has become known as the Cardington A test. This is certainly the most stringent driving test open to those in the business of advanced driver training and testing. Although a number of police driver training schools have been considered to have trained their staff to be the best in the country, it has to be remembered that not all police drivers are trained to these standards, and that most serious advanced courses for them last six weeks or so. If only all drivers could be made to take a six-week advanced course, followed by a refresher every year.

The DSA Pass Plus Scheme

Although it is not strictly an advanced driving test, the Department of Transport, through its Driving Standards Agency, has instigated a recent form of advanced training which is validated by professional instructors. All new drivers who wish to improve their skills, and more importantly wish to gain some form of reduction in their initial insurance premiums, can find a professional driving instructor who is registered with the DSA's Pass Plus Scheme. They are required to take a minimum course of training lasting at least six hours.

In that time they will take a series of lessons on most of the subjects contained in this book. Night driving, bad-weather driving, rural and busy roads, and motorways are all covered. In practice one hour for each of six subjects is nothing like enough. But it is a start, and maybe it – like this book – will encourage new drivers to think about their driving and start to take a pride in it.

The benefits of advanced driving tests

The reasons why people take tests are numerous, but more people would take them if they understood the benefits. As I have explained personally to many drivers over the past forty years that I have been involved in professional driver training, the real benefit of taking any form of driving test is not the actual certificate, the insurance premium, or the badge on the car: the real benefit is the experience of learning and improving your driving skills. If we look at accidents purely statistically, every driver has one bump – of all sorts – every year. Some of them are scarcely reportable, in fact their only importance is that they may even be embarrassing. They include the sort of things that almost every driver does at some time or other, like reversing into the gate post, knocking over some garden furniture lying in the drive, or clumping the pavement with your rear wheel because you turned too sharply. They are momentary aberrations; you know they're wrong, but at the time it becomes less important to think about driving than it does about your breakfast, your job, a football match, what you will wear tonight, or your holiday. They are the result of doing mundane, simple tasks through using autopilot instead of concentrated effort. They occur because at the time we didn't think.

These are the sort of bumps and incidents that statistically happen to every driver once a year. If you are careful, then there are others who aren't and they may probably have your share as well – this year. Insurance claim reports are full of them. Indeed the great majority of road-traffic and vehicle-damage accidents are not caused by the bad and dangerous driver. They occur because the good, safe, and careful driver has a momentary lapse from what is known to be necessary. The snag with the statistical incident is that not all bumps are minor. In some cases the thing that drivers run over in the drive is their own child. In other cases the slip from the brake to the accelerator pedal happens when braking on a motorway. Or perhaps the carelessly opened door knocks a cyclist under another vehicle. The minor error has a catastrophic result!

This is why it is so important that even minor errors that we all make from time to time are monitored and noted. This is why we all need to be aware of our own risk potential. And this is why the

Department of Transport method of marking and noting errors, including minor ones, is so different and so revealing. As is mentioned right at the beginning of this book, driving examiners conduct driving tests and give successful candidates two pieces of paper. One is the pass certificate; the other is the list of minor errors which did not cause a failure but nevertheless still need to have attention paid to them.

Minor errors, if left uncorrected, can easily become part of your driving pattern. Repeated minor errors, especially those noted by a professional advanced driving examiner, such as those who conduct tests for the DIAmond Advanced Motorists scheme, are those which have already become part of your own driving behaviour. Unless and until you make a determined effort to overcome these errors they will almost certainly form part of one or another insurance company's claim forms and reports some time in the future. This is why advanced driving tests are so useful. No matter how experienced you are, no matter how good a driver you have become, you still have weaknesses in your driving pattern that need to be identified and eliminated.

Only then can your driving really be called 'advanced' – better than you were.

This is why advanced driving tests based on the DSA's own system are so important to all of us. This particular test itemizes any repeated minor errors we might make, whether they were caused through lack of knowledge, weak manipulative skills, lack of visual search abilities, or through sheer laziness. Once we know where our risk factor is we can take active steps to avoid putting ourselves in danger when others are likely to turn them to our disadvantage. A minor error, such as failing to check a blind spot, may have no significance at all on the drive we are doing at the moment. But that same error, repeated on a different occasion, can make all the difference between a safe arrival and a collision.

Advanced driving tests, especially when they are repeated annually, enable all of us to know where our weaknesses are, and give us the opportunity to live within our risk potential whilst we learn to conquer it.

Advanced Driving Test Report

CANDIDATES FULL NAME AND ADDRESS

Name

Address

EYESIGHT TEST

- Compliance with the requirements of the Eyesight test. ☐

TEST DATE   TEST TIME

☐☐☐   ☐☐
☐☐☐   ☐☐

VEHICLE DETAILS

Make

Model

Reg. No.

Your driving has been examined on the vehicle detailed above and has/has not reached the standard required.

The examiner has noted the points of failure/ weakness that will require special attention, these may be identified by the following code:

MINOR FAULT –	/
REPEATED MINOR FAULTS –	//
POTENTIALLY DANGEROUS –	X
DANGER ACTUALLY CAUSED –	D

DIAmond ADVANCED EXAMINER (Signature):

CONTROL

- Take proper precautions before starting the engine ☐

- Make proper use of:

  accelerator ☐   clutch ☐   gears ☐

  footbrake ☐   parking/ handbrake ☐   steering ☐

- Move away: safely ☐   under control ☐

- Stop vehicle in an emergency promptly and under control ☐

- Reverse left into a limited opening:

  under control ☐   with proper observation ☐   reasonably accurately ☐

- Reverse right into a limited opening:

  under control ☐   with proper observation ☐   reasonably accurately ☐

- Reverse parking:

  under control ☐   with proper observation ☐   reasonably accurately ☐

- Turn round using forward and reverse gears:

  under control ☐   with proper observation ☐   reasonably accurately ☐

ROAD PROCEDURE

- Make effective use of mirror(s) well before:

  signalling ☐   changing direction ☐   overtaking ☐

  slowing down/stopping ☐

- Give signals by direction indicators/arm:

  where necessary ☐   correctly ☐   properly timed ☐

- Take prompt and appropriate action on all:

  traffic signs ☐   road markings ☐   traffic lights ☐

  signals by traffic controllers ☐   other road users ☐

- Exercise proper care in the use of speed ☐

- Drive at an appropriate speed, avoid undue hesitancy and use safe opportunities to proceed or overtake. ☐

- Follow behind another vehicle at a safe distance ☐

- Act properly at road junctions with regard to:

  speed on approach ☐   observation ☐

  approaching traffic ☐   position before turning right ☐

  right corner cutting ☐   position before turning left ☐

- Deal with vehicles safely when:

  overtaking ☐   meeting ☐   crossing their path ☐

- Position the vehicle correctly:

  during normal driving ☐   exercise lane discipline ☐

- Allow adequate clearance to stationary vehicles ☐

- Take appropriate action at pedestrian crossings ☐

- Select a safe position for normal stops ☐

- Show awareness and anticipation of the actions of:

  pedestrians ☐   cyclists ☐   drivers ☐

Points to remember

- Advanced drivers make fewer minor errors than others.
- Even one minor error can kill a coachload if you do it at the wrong time.
- Repeated minor errors by good drivers still need to be identified.
- Advanced driving is not being better than everyone else, it is being better than you were.
- Advanced driving is knowing what mistakes you make and aiming to eradicate them.
- Passing an advanced driving test whilst on your best behaviour is no good if you don't maintain it.
- The best drivers are those who never stop learning.
- Advanced drivers are continually looking for chances to improve.
- The best drivers are those who actively improve all their skills.

Addresses of Advanced Driver Testing organizations

The Institute of Advanced Motorists
IAM House
359 Chiswick High Road
LONDON W4 4HS
Tel 0181 994 4403

The Royal Society for the Prevention
of Accidents
Advanced Drivers Association
Cannon House
The Priory Queensway
BIRMINGHAM B4 6BS
Tel 0121 200 2461

The DIAmond Advanced Motorists
MasterDriver Club
Safety House
Beddington Farm Road
CROYDON CR0 4XZ
Tel 0181 665 5151

The Driving Standards Agency
The Pass Plus Scheme
Stanley House
Talbot Street
NOTTINGHAM NG1 5GU
Tel 01159 557600

Further details about Skid Training, Four by Four, Off-Road, and Corporate Driver Training can be obtained from

UNIVERSAL DRIVER TRAINING
Brooklands House
65 Park Street
Camberley
SURREY GU15 3PE
Tel 01276 677111

IAM FLEET TRAINING
IAM House
359/365 Chiswick High Road
LONDON W4 4HS
Tel 0181 994 4403

ACCIDENT PROCEDURES

If you are involved in an accident

You *must* stop and exchange vehicle and driver details with other parties who are entitled to them. Arrange hazard lights or triangles to be displayed. Take steps to avoid further collisions, and avoid obstruction if you can. Warn other traffic and switch off all engines.

Call the police and emergency services if anyone is injured or vehicles badly damaged. Do not move the badly injured or allow anyone to smoke near vehicles. Do not remove motorcyclists' helmets, unless it is essential.

Give first aid if you can, and it is needed. Move uninjured people away from the scene and ask for witnesses to remain. Stay at the scene until the emergency services arrive.

Make sure that you exchange details and collect witnesses' names and addresses. Get the drivers' names and full insurance details (insurance company, policy number, and details of cover). You also need to get the name of the registered keeper of each vehicle; this means noting the make, model, and registration numbers of all involved vehicles. Also sketch all vehicle positions immediately prior to the incident, and take photographs, if you can, of the result. Make good notes of the location, time, and weather conditions.

If any involved driver refuses or does not give you the details needed, make sure that the police are informed in person immediately, or within twenty-four hours.

If you witness an accident

Stop and see if you can assist. If you cannot help *go away*.

If you do help, park away from the incident, don't compound it.

Make a note of exact location, if no one else has, find a phone.

Send for the police or emergency services if they are needed.

Return and safeguard the scene. Wait with any injured, comfort them, but don't move them unless it is safe and essential.

If you are not needed, or you see an accident on the other side of a dual carriageway, *do not rubberneck*. So many secondary accidents are caused by people looking at the first one.

Accident Report Form

Date: Time: Place:

Own Vehicle Details	Registration No: Make Model Insurance Company Policy No: Tel No:	Damage
Other Driver's Details	Registration No: Make Model Insurance Details Policy No: Tel No:	Notes or Damage
Other Vehicles Involved	Registration No: Make Model Insurance Details Policy No: Tel No:	Notes or Damage
Witness Details	Name Address Tel No:	Police Officer or Vehicle Nos:

Draw a rough sketch of the scene overleaf or on a separate sheet:

Keep this, or a copy, in the car with you at all times. In the event of any incident make a full record at the time.

10 And All the Rest . . .

This description of the ten most important things that your driving instructor forgot to teach you only touches lightly on the entire subject of driving. I have been learning to drive since my first real lesson when I was eleven years old in 1942. Since then I have driven just about every type of vehicle from the Sinclair C5 to a tank. However I still spend at least thirty to forty thousand miles a year behind the wheel driving on motorways, dual carriageways, at night, in good and bad weather, both in Britain and abroad. I am still learning.

I also spend quite a few hours every week driving sideways and backwards in skid cars and other training vehicles. I occasionally drive round a race circuit or rally track or cut across the country in a 4 × 4 or all-terrain vehicle. I am still learning how to keep my hand in on some of the more exotic skills of vehicle handling.

I mention these additional things just to remind you that driving is a living and growing subject. No one knows all there is to it; and here are a few additional items which I have not had time to look at in detail in the foregoing pages.

Driving colours our lives

Green is normal
Colours affect our lives considerably. We even have to obey traffic lights and road signs according to the colours shown. Our normal behaviour pattern is considered to be a green one. This is the condition we are in when we drive to work or home, or off for the

day. Green is a colour of rest, of contentment, and of feeling all's well with the world. If we start to show excitement and extra interest in what we are doing we are told by psychiatrists that our mood has changed to yellow.

Amber gives a buzz

Our cavemen ancestors got this same feeling when they started to hunt for their supper. They felt they were enjoying themselves. They were about to achieve something really good. This is the same feeling that drivers have when they are in a hurry and are just starting to get the buzz. We like to think we are making better progress than those around us. We overtake whenever we can and we feel that our driving is better than those around us. In fact we know we are superior. If the excitement gets tinged with a touch of fear, the colour of our system begins to turn more towards orange. The hunter got this when his prey came close, or started to put up a fight. We get that same feeling when we shoot over the lights after the green light has changed back to amber – or orange.

Orange is the colour you become when the back of your neck starts to tingle. Treat it as a warning sign in its own right. Fighters and hunters need the adrenalin to rise if they are to cope with the challenge ahead, and this feeling is actually caused by the sudden flow of adrenalin around the body. It helps them to perform better. It helps them to do things they couldn't do normally. From a driving point of view, there are no winners in the battle for road safety. Only losers. Remember that an amber light means stop!

Red rage – road rage

Orange ought to be the furthest we ever get from green. But unfortunately we are all human, and as such we ought to realize that some things can make us red with rage. This is a physical body action, as well as a mental one. Road rage, as it is frequently called, happens when something makes us flip. Have you ever driven (or been driven by someone else) when you have been overtaken as you approach roadworks? The signs have been saying 'Get into the left – single file traffic ahead' for 800 then 600 then 400 and now 200 yards. And still these awful drivers are overtaking us.

What should we do? That's easy to answer in the cold print of a page! Drop back to allow them in. What do you do? Have you *never* been tempted to close the gap between you and the vehicle ahead so that the overtaking car has nowhere to go? Have you never smiled when the overtaking driver has received his come-uppance from someone further ahead who has squeezed them out? Have you never said 'Serves them right!'?

That is road rage or red anger, and you and I get it as much as anyone else. Although we all feel it at times, the advanced and safe driver is the one who can control it. Your emotions play a very heavy part in your driving pattern. You must control them if you are to survive. The secret of how to curb them is to recognize them in the first place. You must know when your colours are taking over your driving and at that point remember that it is not a game, it is the most serious thing you may ever do.

> - **Green is for go when it is safe;**
> - **Amber is for gamblers who don't care; and**
> - **Red is for those who are not fit to be on the road.**

Automatics

Throughout this book I have concentrated on drivers who use a manual gear box. I have pretended to ignore the fact that many drivers prefer to use automatic cars. This is not because it is not intended for drivers of automatic cars, but because the skills of driving have very little to do with the mechanics of the vehicle, and everything to do with what other people see you do. Next time you follow a car, or have one coming towards you, do you worry about what gear they are in? Do you wonder if they have a pre-selector gear box? Or even if they have power steering? Of course not. The only things that matter – as I said at the beginning, is that there are two things that concern a driver, or any other road user about a car. They are: its position; and its speed.

Everything else is academic. For instance, I use an automatic camera for most of my photography. I would hate to use a manual focus and manual exposure control when I'm taking video shots of the family. This is because I want all the automatic bits – the autopilot controls – taken away from me whilst I look through the viewfinder in order to make a decision when to shoot. The same thing applies to driving cars. You avoid the need to think about changing gears. You either let the automatic gearbox on the car do it for you, or you allow the subconscious part of your brain to instruct the automatic physical action of your limbs to move the clutch and gear lever – kinaesthetically.

However, if you do use an automatic car there are a number of questions you might think about:

- Do you use it to its full potential?
- Do you know how to use kick down? or hold?
- Did you know you can fail a test – any driving test, advanced or basic – for misuse of gears even in an automatic?

For the benefit of drivers of automatics, or those who are tempted to buy one, it might be pertinent to give a little bit of additional advice:

Kick down – in a car with a manual gear box, if a lot of extra power is needed all of a sudden – for instance to overtake – you can drop down a gear and accelerate harder. This has the effect of giving extra power and speed just when you need it. In an automatic you cannot normally drop down a gear, but you can 'kick down' the accelerator pedal. This electronically changes down to a lower gear and the accelerator becomes much more powerful for a few moments. Similarly, if you want to stay in a low gear for going down a hill, you can engage the hold position on the gear selector lever which will 'hold' the low gear and keep your speed down instead of letting the car run away too quickly.

Incidentally, it is lack of knowledge of 'kick down' and 'hold' which can cause people who take their driving tests in automatic cars to actually fail the test. The sad thing is that it is most unlikely that L-test candidates will need to overtake on a hill during their test. So the first time that they discover they don't know how to do it is when they are on the road, on their own, and spend a long time over-taking; wondering how other people manage.

Other vehicles

MPVs

Not all new cars are saloons and hatchbacks these days. Many larger families are opting for MPVs. These are the multi-purpose vehicles popularized by the Renault Espace, and much copied by other manufacturers since. If your family is getting bigger, an MPV may well be the answer to a few of your problems. Some people adore the driving position of these. The seating position is way up front and you feel as if you were driving a bus; but for long distance drives they are the answer to most of your problems. And they certainly give you a taste for driving in armchair comfort.

Four-wheel drive

To many people four-wheel-drive vehicles, such as the Land Rover and other military-style vehicles, are strictly for farmers and for galloping around the family estate. However since the advent of such vehicles as the RAV4, Suzukis, and other Frontera-type vehicles they are just as often seen on the roads as they are on the farm. In fact the King's Road area of Chelsea seems to be the natural habitat of most types of them. If you have never driven one it is worth the effort. They are not all expensive. In fact the new Kia Sportage sells for about the same price as a family saloon and gives you quite a lot of fun to drive.

Most of them have an optional four-wheel drive and use a double gear box. You choose the most suitable gear for what you are doing. The idea is that you keep the car in two-wheel normal drive for on the road, you then use four-wheel normal gear drive when the going gets tough and muddy, and you select four-wheel drive low ratio when it gets really sticky and steep.

They are noisy but they are tough and one of their greatest virtues is their very high driving position. This is ideal as it means you can see further ahead when you need to make decisions.

Not all four-wheel-drive vehicles look like tanks. Many of the traditional saloon cars such as Mondeos, Cavaliers, and Peugeot 405 or 406 saloons can be bought in a four-wheel-drive version. The fuel consumption is higher but they keep going in bad weather much longer.

Four-wheel-steer
You can also get cars which steer with all four wheels too. Next time you see a new car advertised with all sorts of gadgets, such as four-wheel-steer, traction control, or whatever, why not pop into your local garage and ask the salesman if you can have a drive? If you have an old Vauxhall Viva and you pop into the local Marinello's to test drive the new Ferrari they may not be keen. But every salesman knows that you are his future customer. The only thing that has not been decided yet is when.

Going abroad by ferry or rail

This subject needs a book all to itself, of course. But if you're thinking of taking your car abroad you may be a bit scared. Have a practice by going to the Isle of Wight on one of their ferries first. Or travel to Ireland where they drive on the same side of the road as we do (and of course on the other side and in the middle as well, occasionally): Eire is one of the most delightful countries in the world to visit and drive round. No one is in a hurry, and you can take your time, because red rage will never get there. No wonder they call it the Emerald Isle, it's the greenest and loveliest place to take a car for your first holiday abroad.

The rail tunnel across to France is also a dream. You don't even need to get out of your car. You just drive over to Folkestone, hop on the rail truck, and forty-five minutes later you're driving well on your way to Disneyworld Paris. And in another five minutes you will probably have remembered that they all drive on the wrong side of the road over there. But don't try it out first in Bournemouth Square for a couple of weeks beforehand just to get some practice in.

Put it all on top

When you do get your first long holiday in the car, if you can't get all your stuff in the boot, you have two options: tell mother-in-law she'll have to walk, or put on a roof rack and possibly a top box too. If you do the latter make sure you get some practice with it first. It will seriously affect your steering and general road holding. Try to put the heavy things in the back of the car and leave the light things for the roof rack and box. Try it all out first on a short trip, before the big day (or week!).

The danger of overloaded vehicles is one that never makes itself known until it is too late. An overcrowded car, a roof rack that you have borrowed from someone else, two suitcases tied on with string, a late rush to catch the overnight ferry; and lots of stop-start driving. This must be the ideal recipe for disaster. First of all check that all the roof rack feet and hooks are securely fixed. Then put any cases or boxes near the centre so that the weight is to the bottom and middle of the rack. Wrap them in plastic sheeting, but this must be done properly otherwise it can flap and act like a sail. Cover the whole load and use rubber spiders or bungees to secure it tightly.

Extra care needs to be taken in high winds, especially when overtaking high-sided vehicles. Remember that your centre of gravity has changed dramatically, and that you are very suscep-tible to strong winds from any direction. Even your fuel consumption will rise drastically. Make allowances for all of it.

Towing a caravan

After a few wild experiences with suitcases, roof racks, and the desperate need for more room you may be tempted to buy a caravan. You might then think of all the times that you have been stuck in traffic jams behind a struggling Metro towing a heavy caravan and you'll think again. But eventually the thought comes back again . . .

Towing a caravan is not difficult. But it does need thinking about, and more than anything else it needs practice. If you're worried about where you can do this, get in touch with the Caravan Club of Great Britain, which arranges early training in the skills of rever-sing, manoeuvring, and general handling. These courses are ar-ranged for weekends, so that you can make it a bit of a break at the same time. Some road safety officers also have similar ideas. They often arrange early season breaks round about Easter or Whitsun for new buyers of caravans. As with every other piece of advice in this book there is only one answer: get as much training – and make it professional – as you can. The most dangerous weekends on the roads are not at Christmas or New Year, they occur at Easter when all the caravanners take to the roads, and in July and August when all the overloaded cars drive well beyond their normal limits. Think – and drive within all your limits.

Car parks and parking meters

The one exercise you can really say goodbye to when you have passed your driving test is the dreaded 'Three-point turn' – or 'Causing the car to face the opposite direction by use of the forward and reverse gears'.

In some countries this actual manoeuvre is illegal; but even if you never actually do this exercise again the practice it gave you will prove invaluable in all your parking and manoeuvring exercises that you will do from now on. The secret of parking soon after you have passed your test is to keep to larger areas and avoid parking in tight spots. But if you keep on trying, you will soon find that you can get into smaller and smaller spaces after all.

As a rough guide, if you want to reverse into a meter bay between two other cars see how much room they have left you. If you have two car lengths, then you can drive in frontwards and shuffle your steering to suit. If the gap is reduced to a car and a half in length, then reversing in is the only viable option. Do it as you did in your driving lessons, aiming at the car behind. Once your front has passed the car ahead you can ignore it and concentrate on filling the gap. Parking at an angle is also relatively easy. The skill is to work out where your front is in relation to the kerb and avoid running into it.

Parking in multi-storey car parks

The most usual problem in multi-storey car parks is the sudden change of lighting from bright daylight to murky gloom. You can only cope with this by putting on your lights, and driving slowly, until such time as your vision accepts what is around you. Try to avoid parking in the dirtiest and darkest corners, especially if you are a lone female. Unfortunately these days some characters do not always have the best intentions. If you have to leave the car parked in a shady spot and you are at all worried as you walk back to it, put all your shopping in one hand, and leave the other hand free to hold the car key. If you are harassed or attacked you can use your key to strike the assailant in the face, between the fingers, in his eyes if you feel like it, or in any soft part of the anatomy. You are only allowed to resist with an equal force to that offered to you, but it is far better to overreact to an attack than submit. Most assailants will run rather than fight, so make as much noise as you can.

Better still park somewhere else, safer, to start with.

Manoeuvring skills

Now that you are able to drive on your own there is one particular and final skill that you can teach and practice yourself. It is the ability to put the rear left-hand tyre of the car on to any particular spot you choose. Select a nice quiet piece of car park to practise. Aim to get your rear left wheel on top of a cigarette packet, or where two white lines cross. Practise this until you can do it anywhere and at any time, and you'll be able to enter and win safe driving rallies, manoeuvring tests, and anything you want.

A final thought and a target to achieve

By the time you have read this book I trust that your driving will be much better. I know you will feel so, but you might like to prove just how good you really are – or could be! Think of parking in a confined space: how good are you? Why not try a car and a quarter space?

How about that as a target for you to achieve by the end of the next six months?

Driver's Psychometric Personality Test

Take a test and see what sort of driver you really are

These tests are designed to discover what sort of driver you really are.

Are you suited to the driving lifestyle that you have, or would you be happier in different circumstances? The following series of questions require you to give an instinctive answer, and not spend time pondering about what you think might be the best answer to give. The more honest you are with your answers, the easier it is to determine exactly what will improve your driving skills.

Place a tick under one of these three options

	Agree	Not Sure	Disagree

Section A

		Agree	Not Sure	Disagree
1	I am a sociable, outgoing sort of person	❑	❑	❑
2	I enjoy meeting new people	❑	❑	❑
3	I like driving to new towns and places	❑	❑	❑
4	I am normally a happy individual	❑	❑	❑
5	I don't like my own company	❑	❑	❑
6	I enjoy showing off in my car	❑		❑

Section B

		Agree	Not Sure	Disagree
7	I am nervous when driving alone	❑	❑	❑
8	I hate heavy and strange traffic	❑	❑	❑
9	My moods change when I am driving	❑	❑	❑
10	I worry about breaking down	❑	❑	❑
11	I don't enjoy driving abroad	❑	❑	❑
12	I am not considered very cheerful	❑	❑	❑

	Agree	Not Sure	Disagree

Section C

		Agree	Not Sure	Disagree
13	I hate driving strange or new vehicles	❑	❑	❑
14	I get irritated when I have to queue	❑	❑	❑
15	I get angry with dangerous overtakers	❑	❑	❑
16	I can't relax on long journeys	❑	❑	❑
17	I hate letting other traffic emerge	❑	❑	❑
18	I occasionally crunch the gears	❑	❑	❑

Section D

		Agree	Not Sure	Disagree
19	I get bored easily	❑	❑	❑
20	I get annoyed with slow drivers	❑	❑	❑
21	I think about work when I am driving	❑	❑	❑
22	Driving is not usually much fun	❑	❑	❑
23	I hate change and new things	❑	❑	❑
24	I worry about time when I am driving	❑	❑	❑

Section E

		Agree	Not Sure	Disagree
25	I am thoughtful of others	❑	❑	❑
26	I prefer to cooperate than compete	❑	❑	❑
27	People like working with me	❑	❑	❑
28	I rarely ever argue a lot at work	❑	❑	❑
29	I hate it when I'm doing nothing	❑	❑	❑
30	I can easily cope with more than one thing at a time	❑	❑	❑

Score as under
Agree +1   Not Sure 0   Disagree −1

Scores: A ❑   B ❑   C ❑   D ❑   E ❑

What sort of driver are you, and what should you do about it?

Section A Introvert or Extrovert
More than 3 points	Take skid car and high-performance courses
Between 3 and 0	Take an advanced driving test
Between 0 and −3	Take a defensive driving course
Less than −3 points	Take a refresher course

Section B Stable or Nervous
More than 3 points	Take a refresher course
Between +3 and 0	Take a defensive driver course
Between 0 and −3	Take an advanced driving test
Less than −3 points	Take the skid car course

Section C Serious or Flippant
More than 3 points	Take a defensive driver course
Between 3 and 0	Take an advanced driving test
Between 0 and −3	Take a skid car course
Less than −3 points	Take the high performance course

Section D Stressed or Relaxed
More than 3 points	Take a defensive driving course
Between 3 and 0	Take an advanced driving test
Between 0 and −3	Take a skid car course
Less than −3 points	Take a refresher course

Section E Reliability
More than 3 points	Take a skid car course
Between 3 and 0	Take a high performance course
Between 0 and −3	Take an advanced driving test
Less than −3 points	Take a defensive driving course

Did you do well?

Find out here.

Check all the advice you have been given. If the advice is consistent in four out of the five sections, then you need to seriously think about applying to take the course or test which is advised for you. If you are told to do something two or three times, and other things as well, it could be that you need to have your driving check tested for consistency. In any case, taking an advanced driving test will clearly indicate what you ought to do to ensure your driving skills suit the occasion – at all times.

Are You Really a Good Driver

0 1 2 3 4 5

Do you like driving in strange towns?
Do you enjoy showing off in your car?
Do you ever use your car as a weapon?
Do you ever get irritated when you have to queue?
Do you find driving lots of fun?

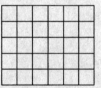

Are you considerate of other people?
Do you consider yourself an aggressive driver?
Do you hate being late for appointments?
Can you cope with more than one thing at a time?
Is it difficult to distract you when you are busy?

Do you enjoy high-speed driving?
Do you enjoy driving in fog and the dark?
Do you enjoy driving in snow and on ice?
Do you ever try to get your car to skid?
Do you think you are a very good driver?

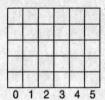

Do you mix well with all kinds of people?
Are you an extrovert in your car?
Are you always alert, even after long drives?
Do you find you get a buzz at high speed?
Do you start your journeys late and still make up time?

0 1 2 3 4 5

Score each of the above on a scale of 0–5
0 = Not at all
1 = Not much
2 = Sort of
3 = Yes, but . . .
4 = Definitely
5 = Absolutely

Your score [　　]

If you scored between:

0–20	**You need re-training**
21–40	**You should take a Defensive Driving Course**
41–60	**You need to take an Advanced Driving Test**
61–80	**You should take Skid Car training**
81–98	**You should take a Hi-Performance course**
99–100	**You don't need training – just a wooden box.**

NOTES

NOTES

NOTES

NOTES

NOTES

NOTES

NOTES

NOTES